THE SURVIVAL GUIDE TO COOKING IN THE Student Kitchen

and the house-sharing experience!

Susan Crook

foulsham
LONDON • NEW YORK • TO

foulsham

The Publishing House, Bennetts Close, Cippenham,
Slough, Berkshire, SL1 5AP, England

Foulsham books can be found in all good bookshops and direct from
www.foulsham.com

ISBN: 978-0-572-03451-1

Copyright © 1995, 1998 and 2008 W. Foulsham & Co. Ltd

Cover photograph © Superstock

A CIP record for this book is available from the British Library

Wyman Ltd, Reading

Contents

Introduction

Kitchen survival isn't likely to be top of most people's anxiety list when they leave home for the first time, but eventually gnawing hunger will take over. Man – and woman – cannot live by lager and crisps alone.

Moving away from home, whether it's to university or to work, may be your first experience of cooking since you followed the Blue Peter recipe for peppermint creams many years ago. Mum was probably around to help you then, but now it's just you and your housemates, struggling to survive in what may feel like a hostile kitchen.

For the first time you're responsible for a home and a budget and how well you handle both will make a huge difference to your experience of student life. All you need is a manual to hold your hand through the initial assault course. This book is designed to help you through the initial challenges so that you can get the most out of shared living. It will help you stick to a budget, organise the cleaning, feed yourself instantly, impress your mates with sumptuous dinners and host memorable parties.

Start with the easier options and you'll soon learn and improve. But don't be afraid to ask someone (including your parents) who's already been there and done that for advice. And, most importantly, don't go mad on spending at the beginning of term when your purse is full; you can always splash out at the end of term if you have been able to save – but if the money runs out early on then you could be in dire straits.

Notes on the recipes

- Where ingredients are given in metric, imperial and cup measures, use only one set per recipe – don't swap around.
- Wash all fresh produce before using and peel where appropriate.
- Eggs are medium unless otherwise stated.
- All spoon measures are level unless otherwise stated.
- When a handful is called for, use as much of the ingredient as you can comfortably hold in your hand without dropping it all over the floor.
- Can sizes are approximate.

1 A caring, sharing household

It all seems desperately exciting as you pack up your posters, pots and pans, wave goodbye to your tearful family and head for a home where you and a bunch of like-minded friends can do anything you like. But it can happen that those rosy dreams of shared living disappear under a pile of dirty dishes and rows about who had the last of the milk! So be realistic, plan ahead and don't be afraid to compromise – this is about sharing, after all.

Planning

Once you've decided who you're going to live with and where, start to sort out the details of how you're going to live. Do this simple multiple-choice test together and take a majority decision on 1, 2 or 3. Then see below for how to put each one into practice.

How do you want to organise the cooking?

1   All cook as a group.
2   Take turns to cook for each other.
3   All cook separately.

Your choice
1   You've picked the cheapest and most fun way of getting fed, but it does involve everyone being prepared to pull their weight and come up with recipes to suit all tastes and an agreed budget.
2   You're giving yourself more freedom to experiment and there won't be other cooks interfering. This system is also fairly flexible as not every member of the household will need to join in every time.
3   This does give you total freedom, but you could end up with a rather unfriendly fridge full of individually named milk bottles and initialled eggs. There also tends to be a lot of waste – so it's more expensive.

How do you want to organise the shopping?

1 All shop together.
2 Buy the basics communally and buy food for the evening meal when it's your turn to cook it.
3 Buy the basics communally and the food separately.

Your choice

1 It's unlikely that you'll all be able to go on every shopping trip, so you'll have to rely on one or two people getting enough food for the week. You'll need to have a good idea of what you all like.
2 This is more practical. It could be tricky if one person wants to cook chicken while someone else is churning out variations on Spaghetti Lentilese, but it should even out in the end. It allows for some people not to get involved in communal food at all.
3 It's worth having a common fund for household necessities like washing powder and bills (see Chapter 3 on pages 17–19) for hints on budgets and kitties). If you seriously think you should each buy your own basics such as loo rolls, then you really shouldn't be living together.

Who's going to wash up?

1 We'll have a rota.
2 Whoever cooks that night.
3 We'll all do our own as we go along.

Your choice

Doing the washing up (or, more accurately, not doing it) causes more tension in shared households than almost any other issue. Nothing is more frustrating than rushing home to make a cup of tea before settling down to your favourite TV programme only to discover that there isn't a clean mug in the house. All the recipes in this book are designed for minimal washing up.

1 Draw up a rota, stick it on the wall and stick to it. Work out how many weeks there are in the term and allocate accordingly in strict rotation. Be reasonable with each other – if you all have a quick meal then go out for the night, you can't expect one person to stay behind doing the washing up! But it should be done by the time someone starts cooking the next day. Everyone will have to be helpful about swapping, too, if someone's away for the night or weekend or going out.

2 This is quite harsh and you may feel that once you've cooked for the night then the last thing you want to do is go back into the kitchen to wash up. In that case, go with the rota above.

3 If you're cooking separately then you must also do your own washing up. And no trying to sneak your pile of dirty dishes and pans under someone else's – it won't win you any friends.

How are you going to get the cleaning done?

1 We'll have a rota.

2 We'll draw straws on who cleans what and swap round each term.

3 When the mess gets really bad we'll all spontaneously burst into an energetic round of cleaning.

Your choice

1 Another rota. Well, if you're going to have a go at one you may as well have another. Decide what needs cleaning (nothing should need cleaning more than once a week) and build your rota around that. The main areas are kitchen, bathroom, vacuuming and tidying.

2 Less complicated to organise than a rota but it does mean that one housemate gets stuck with scrubbing the loo for a term/month, in which case the unlucky person gets a nicer task next time.

3 Dream on!

What are you going to do if one or more person doesn't pull their weight?

1 It won't happen.
2 Ignore it and hope they go away.
3 Face the problem head on.

Your choice

1 Oh yes it will!
2 This could make the problem worse – freeloaders will just get used to having an easy time.
3 Try these methods:

- Point out that they are becoming very unpopular.
- Communal shouting – if you all shout at them then it doesn't turn into a personal argument.
- Dump all the washing up someone should have done under his or her duvet.
- Don't cook for them – even if they're sitting at the table with everyone else.
- If they are causing real tension, ask them to leave.

(But do remember these are drastic measures – hopefully it won't get this far.)

Basic equipment

If, like the majority of students, you rent furnished accommodation privately, then your landlord should supply some household necessities. However, what comes with the house and what you'd like to have will probably be poles apart. You'll also find that three people in the house will have kettles while no one has brought a toaster. Tick off what you've got from the list below then fill in gaps by:

- Dropping hints to your parents.
- Swapping with friends who have all toasters and no kettles, etc.
- Picking up things you need in the supermarket or pound shop.

Kitchen essentials

Large frying pan
Small frying pan
Large saucepan
Medium saucepan
Small saucepan
Colander and/or sieve (strainer)
Baking (cookie) sheet
Roasting tin
Grill (broiler) pan
Large plates
Side plates
Pudding/cereal bowls
Mugs
Knives
Forks
Dessert spoons
Teaspoons
Tablespoons
Small sharp knife
Bread knife
Potato peeler
Can opener

Scissors
Two wooden spoons
Draining spoon
Fish slice
Small whisk
Casserole dish (Dutch oven)
Mixing bowl
Measuring jug
Chopping board
Grater
Toaster
Corkscrew and bottle opener
Kettle
Oven gloves
Tea towels
Hand towel
Dusters
Dish cloths
Washing-up brush
Washing-up liquid
Pan scourers
Draining rack

2 Stocks and shares

The kitchen is equipped and the rotas are pinned to the wall, but the cupboard is looking bare. Whether you're cooking together or on your own, you will need to start building up a collection of basics everyone can share.

The list below should form the basis of your first trip to the supermarket. Buying everything on it between you won't cost the earth and some things will last all year. As a guide, buy large sizes of items you use lots – tea, coffee, cereals, etc. – and items that won't perish, but buy small sizes of things that will be used only infrequently or in small quantities – chilli powder, herbs, etc. Try out supermarkets' own brands too – they're usually much cheaper than well-known brands.

The basics

- margarine (check that it's suitable for cooking – look on the packet)
- jam (fruit conserve)
- caster (superfine) sugar (it can be used in drinks and for cooking)
- coffee
- tea bags
- frozen peas
- salt
- pepper
- dried mixed herbs
- chilli powder
- curry powder
- garam masala and/or ground cumin
- tomato ketchup (catsup)
- mayonnaise

- vinegar (preferably cider, red wine or white wine or use malt)
- good-quality vegetable oil (e.g. sunflower or corn)
- olive oil
- plain (all-purpose) flour
- peanut butter (instant protein!)
- vegetable stock cubes
- dried milk powder (non-fat dry milk)
- soy sauce
- Worcestershire sauce
- a small tub of grated Parmesan cheese
- made mustard
- foil
- clingfilm (plastic wrap)
- washing-up liquid
- bathroom/kitchen cleaner
- bin liners
- disposable dish cloths
- kitchen paper (paper towels)
- loo rolls

and don't forget fresh bread and milk!

Beyond the basics

You may find your attempt at communal living works out so well that you're able to expand the house shopping list to include items that you all cook with on a regular basis. The most common ingredients used in this book are:

- canned tomatoes
- garlic
- onions
- cheese
- bacon
- carrots
- potatoes
- baked beans
- red lentils
- brown rice
- spaghetti
- pasta shapes

Finding fresh foods

There's no point wasting your culinary efforts on questionable meat or iffy potatoes, so:

Don't buy
- Fish that has dull scales and eyes or smells fishy (odd, that).
- Dented cans of meat or fish – their price may have been reduced but the contents will have been traumatised (fruit and veg are okay, though).
- Meat with a brown tinge.
- Fruit and veg with a label saying 'ripe' – it means overripe.

Do buy
- Special offers of foods you use regularly.
- Cheap bags of fruit and veg at the market, but throw out any rotten ones as soon as you get home or they'll ruin the lot.
- Crisp-looking veg without dark brown spots.
- Bread that's still slightly warm (though beware of squashing it on the way home and don't expect it to last long!).

Chilling out

All food will last longer if kept cool until ready to use, but fridge space will be limited so don't keep everything in there. Use your kitchen space sensibly and don't keep any foods too close to the cooker. If you have a larder cupboard with ventilation, use it!

In the fridge
- milk
- veg (at the bottom)
- food from opened cans decanted into covered containers
- raspberries
- eggs (in the door only)
- cheese
- meat and fish
- mayonnaise
- pesto sauce
- salad

Out of the fridge
- rice
- pasta
- all other fruit
- onions
- potatoes
- bread (it goes stale quicker in the fridge)
- seasonings
- garlic
- tea and coffee
- flour and other dry goods

Keep all raw foods (especially meat) well wrapped and low down in the fridge so it can't drip on to cooked food.

Respect your fridge

Keep an eye on the temperature – if the food you take out has ice crystals in it, it's set too cold; but if your milk goes off in a day or so then it needs to be changed to a colder setting (or you bought dodgy milk). Keep the fridge clean – wipe up spills as they occur – and keep all smelly foods well wrapped. If the fridge starts to smell, clear out everything, switch it off and let it defrost (unless it's self-defrosting). Here's how:

- If you have frozen food you want to keep, wrap it in plastic bags, then in blankets or duvets, until the freezer is switched on again.
- Have lots of bowls and towels ready to catch the water.
- If the freezer section is really iced up, sit a bowl of hot water in it to get the ice moving quicker. Keep changing the hot water.
- Wash the inside with warm water that has had a tablespoonful of bicarbonate of soda (baking soda) dissolved in it.
- Wipe round, then leave to dry with the door open.

The dating game

Just about everything you buy in the supermarket these days has a date on it. The label may say:

- Display until
- Best before
- Sell by
- Use by

'Display until' and 'sell by' aren't really your problem; they're guidance for the shop. 'Best before' means that beyond that date the quality of the food may have deteriorated a little, but it should still be safe to eat. 'Use by' means what it says, and you would ignore that date at your peril! Supermarkets will want to sell foods that are on or just approaching their sell-by dates and there are often bargains to be had; just make sure you'll be using the food before the use-by date.

However, most of these dates are playing very safe and a bag of salad a day past its date won't kill you; but do be especially careful with meat, eggs and processed foods such as pâté and margarine.

If you find you're often throwing away food because it's past its date, then you need to review how much food you're buying each week; don't over-shop.

You are what you eat

This isn't a lecture about eating healthily, but when you start thinking about what you're going to be buying and eating, spare a thought for what you're actually putting into your body. It stands to reason that the better the fuel is, the better the engine will run. There's a lot of complicated info around on what you should and shouldn't be eating but, unless you're studying nutrition, don't worry too much about it.

Just bear in mind that the majority of your diet should be based on starchy carbohydrates (i.e. stodgy foods such as pasta, bread, potatoes and rice – and brown really is best) and fresh veg/fruit, with a small amount of protein (meat, fish, eggs, cheese) and very little fat, salt or sugar. Think of it as a pyramid of pleasure.

- **Nice stuff:** *salty/sugary/fatty foods* – eat little.
- **Expensive stuff:** *meat, fish, eggs, cheese* – have some daily.
- **Healthy stuff:** *vegetables, fruit, pulses* – eat lots.
- **Filling stuff:** *bread, pasta, rice, potatoes* – eat lots.

3 Spend! Spend! Spend!

Most students have very little money. This is a fact of life, so get used to it before we go any further. What you need to work out is how to make the best of what you have so the majority of it can be spent on having fun.

Shopping and eating together will work out cheaper, though it can be more tempting to splash out on luxuries if the cost is shared than if all the money is coming directly from your own pocket.

Whichever way you choose to organise your household, you'll need to sort out a way of splitting the cost – even if you're only sharing the electricity bill.

Where is all my money going?

You'll ask this question a lot. These are the main areas of essential expenditure:

- rent
- electricity bill
- gas bill
- food
- phone bill
- travel

Work out how much you're spending a week on each and it should give you an idea of how much money you'll have over to spend on the nicer things of life – not to mention books and equipment.

All the recipes here have been written with an eye on economy, but don't forget to budget for meals away from home.

Here kitty, kitty

You'll need to put aside a fixed sum each week to cover the shared household bills – electricity, gas, phone, TV rental, food and non-food essentials like bin liners.

The best way to do this is with a kitty. Each of you pays your share each week, either to a jar kept under someone's bed or, if you want to be sophisticated, set up a household bank account. Both methods involve you having to trust another member of your household enough to look after the money/keep the cheque book. If you don't, best not get involved with a kitty system. If the slacker in your house is claiming impecunity, don't let them get away with not paying. Give them a date – maybe the first of the month – to cough up by. If they still don't pay up, padlock the fridge and remove their light bulbs. If they aren't paying for food and electricity, they don't want them, right?

The main advantage of the kitty is that it helps you budget over the term – and if there's any cash left at the end of term you can have a party! On the downside, it can lead to questions about who's spending money on what, and there's usually one person who treats it as a loan system for emergency drinking sessions.

An alternative way to organise the household budget is to buy the bits and pieces you need and keep a tally in a book. Work out the totals once a month, so the people who are more efficient about buying bread, milk, etc. aren't out of pocket for too long. Have a whip-round for big bills.

If you decide not to have a kitty, then it's up to you to keep control of your budget so you're able to pay the bills – even if they come in the last week of term.

Keeping the cost down

There are endless ways to cut corners and live cheaply. Here are my Top Ten money-spinning greats:

- Check out your local market and make it the focus of shopping trips. Fruit, veg, eggs, cheese and loads of other things can be bought at a fraction of supermarket prices.

- When you do have to go to the supermarket, go at the end of the day when fresh produce nearing its sell-by date is marked down.

- Keep an eye on supermarket special offers – particularly own brands. They often do 'three for the price of two' deals, which are a bargain for essential items.

- Don't ever buy ready-packed supermarket fruit and veg – you're saving simply by picking up a bag and filling it yourself.

- Supermarket-prepared food like pizza and lasagne is often cheaper if you buy it frozen rather than from the chill cabinet.

- Collect money-off vouchers that come through the door or fall out of newspapers.

- Buy thin-cut bread. No one will notice the difference and you get a few more slices for your money. If it goes stale, sprinkle a slice with a drop of water and then toast it.

- Remember that electricity costs more than gas, so if you need hot water for cooking, heat it in a saucepan rather than in the electric kettle. In fact, if you have a gas hob don't bother at all with an electric kettle; one that sits on the hob will be cheaper to buy and run and can heat only the amount of water you need each time.

- If you're cooking something that needs the oven, a casserole for example, do baked potatoes and veg in the oven too to save fuel.

- Buy seasonally. Even though you can buy just about any fresh produce throughout the year, it will be much cheaper during its natural season. Strawberries, for instance, cost a fortune in January and about a tenth of the price in July – and taste much better too.

4 But I can't even boil an egg!

If the last thing you cooked was that Blue Peter recipe for peppermint creams a decade ago, despair not. Basic cooking is a cinch. Just bear this simple formula in mind:

$$\text{raw food} + \text{heat} = \text{delicious hot food}$$

and you can't go wrong. It's just a question of knowing how to apply which heat to what food.

The main cooking methods are boiling, steaming, oven baking, roasting, frying and grilling (broiling).

Boiling

You'll need a saucepan big enough to cook the quantity of food (see page 25 for guidelines on quantities) plus enough room for it to cook properly. The basic principle is to bring a saucepan of water to the boil and then add the food. Continue boiling until it's cooked.

Pasta: Use a big saucepan (the pasta will need to move around while it's cooking), fill it two-thirds full with water and bring to the boil. Add a dash of oil and a pinch of salt. Pour in the pasta and stir it with a wooden spoon. Turn the heat down so the water just simmers (i.e. bubbles gently) and stir occasionally during cooking. Don't cover the pan or it will boil over. Pasta usually takes about 8 minutes to cook; wholemeal pasta will take a little longer. To check if it's done, lift a piece out with the wooden spoon, run it under the cold tap and eat it; you don't want pasta to be too soggy – it needs a bit of texture.

Eggs: Put the eggs into a saucepan of cold water. Add a burnt match to the water (it sounds mad but for some reason it helps to stop the shell cracking) and bring to the boil. Once the water is boiling, let it simmer for 3 minutes for a firm white and soft yolk, 5 minutes for a firm yolk. These times should work for medium-sized eggs; you will need a little less time for small eggs or more time for large ones.

Rice: White rice is tricky to cook; brown is much better behaved, as well as being higher in fibre. Boil a kettle of water and meanwhile gently heat a tablespoonful of oil in the bottom of a saucepan. Add the rice to the oil and stir it round for a minute (this helps to stop it sticking). Add the water and bring to the boil, stir once, then turn down the heat. It should take about 8–10 minutes to cook for white, up to 30 minutes for brown. Don't stir rice too much as it will go mushy. Drain through a sieve (strainer) and rinse with boiling water, then drain again.

Potatoes: A lot of the goodness is just under the skin, so don't peel them unless you plan to mash them. Just scrub them and take out the blemishes and bumpy bits. Chop into smallish pieces and cover with cold water. Bring to the boil and allow 10–15 minutes' cooking time until a knife goes through easily. Baby new potatoes should be put in boiling water and cooked for 8–10 minutes. For mash, drain thoroughly and add a splash of milk, a knob of margarine, salt and pepper and mash with a potato masher or a fork until soft and fluffy.

Vegetables: Peel and chop the vegetables, if necessary. Bring just enough water to cover them to the boil in a saucepan and add the vegetables. Simmer for just long enough until they are tender: green vegetables (peas, broccoli, etc.) will need less time than root vegetables (carrots, turnips, etc.).

Steaming

This is the best way to cook almost all vegetables (potatoes are better boiled) because it keeps in all the goodness and colour – and the flavour. You don't need a high-tech steamer – a metal colander over a saucepan of boiling water which is then covered with the saucepan lid does the job just as well. Many woks come with a steaming 'shelf' too. Cooking times are slightly longer than with boiling, but are justified by the results.

Broccoli: Rinse and chop into small pieces, using the stalks as well as the florets. Steam for 5 minutes.

Carrots: Top, tail and scrape or peel. Cut into slices a matchstick thick. Steam for about 3 minutes.

Green beans: Rinse, top and tail. Cut into two or three pieces if liked or leave whole. Steam for 3 minutes.

Greens: Remove the tough stalks and outer leaves. Rinse, slice thinly and pack into the colander or steamer. Bring the water underneath to the boil, put a lid over the steamer and steam for 5 minutes.

Oven baking

It's a good idea to pre-heat the oven for 5 minutes before putting the food in, especially when cooking cakes or biscuits (cookies). If you're using the oven, it's worth cooking more than one dish at the same time to save fuel. But remember, if the oven is filled with food it will all take slightly longer to cook. A warm oven is also useful for keeping food hot while you wait for everyone to come back from the pub.

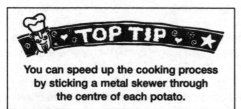

You can speed up the cooking process by sticking a metal skewer through the centre of each potato.

Potatoes: Choose large ones and give them a good scrub. Score the longest side with a sharp knife (to stop the potato splitting and to make it easier to cut open when cooked). Put in an oven preheated to 190°C/ 375°F/gas 5/fan oven 170°C for 1 hour. However, potatoes will also bake very happily at virtually any temperature so you can pop them in when you are cooking something else – just allow more time at a lower temperature or less time if the oven is set higher.

Apples: Core cooking (tart) apples from top to bottom using a sharp knife and place in a shallow baking tin. Fill the hole with dried fruit, nuts or muesli, sprinkle a tablespoonful of sugar and a tablespoonful of water over each apple and bake for 30 minutes at around 190°C/375°F/gas 5/fan oven 170°C.

Roasting

This is like baking except that the food cooks in fat or oil.

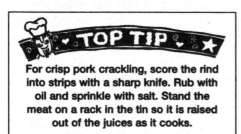

For crisp pork crackling, score the rind into strips with a sharp knife. Rub with oil and sprinkle with salt. Stand the meat on a rack in the tin so it is raised out of the juices as it cooks.

Meat: a joint is expensive but it makes a delicious treat. Allow 225–300 g/ 8–12 oz per person if the meat has bones in and 100– 175 g (4–6 oz) per person if it hasn't. Choose a joint of meat that looks fresh and lean. Leave on any string to hold its shape until it's cooked. Wipe with kitchen paper (paper towels) and put in a roasting tin. Rub over with a little oil unless it has a coating of fat. Preheat the oven to 190°C/375°F/gas 5/fan oven 170°C. Roast in the middle of the oven for 25 minutes per 450 g/1 lb, plus an extra 25 minutes if you want it well done. Reduce by 5 minutes per 450 g/1 lb if you like it pink in the middle of a lamb or beef joint. Pork must be thoroughly cooked; the meat shouldn't be at all pink.

Poultry: Nothing is easier to roast than a chicken, and it's cheap too. Make sure it's completely thawed if frozen. Rinse the chicken and take out any bits (the giblets) in the body cavity. Put the chicken in a roasting tin and rub with oil. Preheat the oven to 190°C/375°F/gas 5/fan oven 170°C. Roast for 20 minutes per 450 g/1 lb plus an extra 20 minutes.

Potatoes: Roast tatties are one of life's great pleasures. Peel more potatoes than you think you need, then boil for 5 minutes. Drain, then chuck back into the saucepan and shake for about 10 seconds to roughen their surfaces so they will brown and crisp. Heat 2 tablespoonfuls of oil in a large roasting tin. Add the potatoes and roll them around until coated in oil. Put in the top of the oven while cooking the meat. Baby new potatoes can be roasted too. Simply rinse them, roll them around in an oiled baking tin and cook as above.

Vegetables: Root vegetables like parsnips and carrots can be roasted in exactly the same way as potatoes, but you don't need to shake them to roughen the surfaces.

Frying

Pour as thin a layer as possible of vegetable oil into your frying pan and heat it gently (sausages and bacon won't need fat, though, as they have plenty of their own). Whatever you're frying, keep an eye on it – there's a thin line between frying and burning.

Fry sausages, bacon, chicken, vegeburgers, beefburgers, mushrooms, eggs and sliced courgettes (zucchini). Frying chicken pieces, sausages or any thick foods takes around 20–30 minutes over a low to medium heat. Don't have the heat too high or they'll be raw inside and burnt outside.

How to fry the perfect egg: Get the oil hot, but not hissing. Crack in the egg (in a cup first if you're not very good at it) and stop it spreading too far by pushing the white back towards the yolk with a fish slice. As the white cooks, spoon the hot oil across the yolk and on to that bit of white round it that never cooks. Use the fish slice to dish it out.

Grilling

Grilling (broiling) works like frying by cooking food one side at a time, but from above, not below, and without the cooking oil. Again, watch the grill very carefully. Always have the grill hot before putting the food under it.

Sausages: Turn frequently under a medium heat for about 20 minutes, depending on size. Don't prick them.

Bacon: Make little cuts along the fatty edge of the bacon (this stops it curling up) and grill for about 4 minutes on each side.

Courgettes (zucchini) and aubergines (eggplants): Top and tail, then slice thinly from top to bottom. Brush both sides of each slice with oil; if you don't have a pastry brush use a scrunched-up piece of kitchen paper (paper towel) dipped in oil. Grill for 3 minutes on each side.

Red, green and yellow (bell) peppers: Top and tail, cut in half vertically and remove the white bits and seeds inside. Grill, skin-sides up, until the skin blackens. Pop the pepper pieces into a plastic bag or wrap in foil for 10 minutes (this loosens the skin). Peel off the skin and serve with olive oil or salad dressing (see Salads in Chapter 6 on pages 40–44). Delicious.

Microwaving

I haven't mentioned microwave cooking before because the chances are that you are already familiar with using one, if only to heat up the kind of ready-prepared meals I am trying to steer you away from (they're expensive and often not very nutritious).

However, since most student kitchens have a microwave oven, here are a few hints:

- Metal and microwaves don't mix. Never put anything metal in the microwave, including plates with metal decoration or aluminium foil.

- Allow all microwaved foods to stand for a minute (the cooking process continues for a while after the timer has gone off).

- Pasta and rice don't cook particularly well in the microwave – and anyway take almost as long as when you boil them.

- A large potato can be baked in about 5 minutes. Prick the skin all over with a fork, rub the skin with butter or oil and microwave on High.

- A rasher of bacon will cook (though it won't brown and crisp) in 1 minute on High (allow 1½ minutes for two). Place the bacon on a plate and cover with a sheet of kitchen paper (paper towel) so it doesn't spatter.

- Soften butter or margarine that has come rock hard out of the fridge. Put it in a small dish and microwave on Low for just a minute at a time until it's soft enough to spread on your bread or toast. Keep an eye on it though, because it will go from hard to liquid very quickly.

Flavouring

Any dish can be improved by being well seasoned. This usually means adding salt and pepper after cooking until it tastes as you want it. Chilli powder, dried mixed herbs, Worcestershire sauce, soy sauce, mustard and curry powder are store cupboard basics that can add masses of flavour. 'Wet' seasonings (mustard, soy sauce, fresh herbs, etc.) can be added after cooking; dry ones (dried herbs, chilli powder, etc.) will need to be cooked with the dish. Just add a little to start with, then more if you need to.

Quantities

Very few student kitchens are equipped with sophisticated weighing scales, but the majority of recipe books call for 100 g of this or 13 fl oz of that.

Ignore all that stuff – in this book virtually all quantities are given as handfuls or easy-to-measure portions. Don't forget that tsp = teaspoon and tbsp = tablespoon.

If your first attempts at cooking results in a handful of rice between six or enough spaghetti to feed the five

TOP TIP

As a guide, rice and pasta double in size once cooked, so if you normally eat about 4 tbsp when cooked, use 2 tbsp raw and so on.

thousand, next time stop and think about how much food you'd like to see on your plate.

Rewriting the recipes

Once you master the basics of cooking, don't be afraid to experiment. A recipe is a guideline, not a commandment. There are no hard and fast rules in this book – if you want something spicy, add chilli; if you've got lots of potatoes sitting around, boil some up and chuck them into the curry/omelette/soup that's on the go.

I've tried to give alternatives in the recipes that follow, but if it says 'add chopped bacon' and you haven't any or don't eat it, try chopped mushrooms or (bell) peppers instead. There are as many variations as there are people to cook them.

Getting saucy

The most easily varied recipes of all are the two basic sauces that will keep you happily fed for years – white sauce and tomato sauce. Each one can be the basis of many different dishes and can be poured over cooked pasta, rice, baked potatoes or even toast. They can also be diluted with water to make soup.

White sauce

Melt 1 tbsp of margarine or vegetable oil in a saucepan. Stir in 1 tbsp of flour. Whisk in 300 ml/½ pt/1¼ cups of milk. Bring to the boil, whisking all the time. Season well with salt and pepper.

Cheese sauce: Add a handful of grated cheese with the salt and pepper.

Mushroom sauce: Fry a handful of sliced mushrooms in the margarine/oil before adding the flour and milk.

Leek/onion sauce: Fry one thinly sliced leek/onion in the margarine/oil before adding the flour and milk.

Tomato sauce

Peel and chop an onion. Fry in 1 tbsp of oil until it's transparent, then add a 400 g/14 oz/large can of chopped tomatoes. Boil rapidly for 5 minutes. Season with salt, pepper and a pinch of dried mixed herbs.

Chilli sauce: Add ½ tsp chilli powder to the sauce when you season it.

Italian sauce: Fry a handful of sliced mushrooms with the onion and go heavy with the herbs.

Tuna sauce: Drain a small (200 g/7 oz) can of tuna and add with the tomatoes.

Bacon sauce: Chop two rashers (slices) of bacon and fry with the onion.

5 Exam crisis and feeding yourself instantly

You know that feeling… starving hungry, but not a second to spare from last-minute revision/all-night essay frenzy or, heaven forbid, actually enjoying yourself. It's time to resort to easy food – to open a few cans or head for the supermarket chill cabinet.

It is really important to eat properly; if you're starving hungry in an exam you won't be able to think straight. If you really can't face food, take some glucose tablets into the exam room with you and eat them regularly. This will keep up your blood sugar level, helping to keep your brain ticking over at a reasonable pace.

During my finals I lived on pasties, salad and samosas from the Indian supermarket round the corner – all instant foods. Try not to buy prepared ready meals – they cost a fortune and aren't very good for you. Ditto takeaways. A friend of mine revised in a curry house every night for a

Don't forget the simple sandwich. Make huge ones with any filling you like. Use a variety of loaves, rolls and pitta breads. Add salad bits for vitamins and minerals.

month. Having seen the size of his gut and his overdraft afterwards I wouldn't recommend it. But there's no harm in spoiling yourself once in a while!

Supermarket sweeps

In times of crisis the supermarket will help you – as long as you don't start helping yourself to overpriced selections of Indian and Chinese nibbles, chicken tikka or prepared tomato sauce for pasta (my tomato sauce recipe on page 26 tastes just as good at a third of the price).

The best value comes from vegetable dishes and basic things like cheese and tomato pizza that you can add your own toppings to.

Here are a few more ideas:

- Little packs of ready-to-stir-fry vegetables.
- Sachets of rice with bits in – Thai or Indian-style are good and don't cost much. Add some frozen veg and soy sauce or mango chutney.
- Oriental noodle soup – for very little money you get a pack of noodles that takes 3 minutes to cook, plus a sachet of flavouring. Add a few frozen peas or any cooked leftover vegetables in the fridge.
- Simple chill cabinet meals-for-one like lasagne or cauliflower cheese – they are a very good buy.
- Tins of vegetable curry, ratatouille or stir-fry. Serve with rice noodles (they take only minutes to cook).
- Baked beans with meatballs or sausages – a cheap filler.
- Frozen crispy pancakes.
- Frozen chilli or curry with rice.
- Frozen pizza – cheaper than the chilled variety.
- Houmous, taramasalata or tzatziki – Greek dips that can be served with pitta bread, tortilla chips, cucumber sticks and carrots.

Store cupboard standbys

If your store cupboard is reasonably well stocked you should be able to rustle up the following recipes in minutes. All produce minimal washing up and serve one (it's every man for himself in an exam crisis).

Baked bean deluxe

SERVES 1

2 slices of bread

Butter or margarine

Marmite

A handful of grated cheese

A small (200 g/7 oz) can of baked beans

1 Toast the bread, butter it and spread with Marmite.

2 Top with the cheese and grill (broil) until bubbling.

3 Meanwhile, heat the beans. Pour the beans over the toast.

Cheese and egg toasties

SERVES 1

Margarine or butter

2 slices of bread

A small handful of grated cheese

1 or 2 eggs

A toasted sandwich maker

1 Preheat the sandwich maker.

2 Butter the bread and put one slice buttered-side down in the bottom bit.

3 Sprinkle on the cheese, then break the egg on top.

4 Split the yolk with a knife (this is the tricky bit) so it runs equally into each section.

5 Top with the other slice of bread, buttered-side up, and cook.

TOP TIP

If you don't have a sandwich maker, make up a cheese sandwich, beat the egg in a shallow dish and soak the sandwich in it on both sides until completely covered. Fry in a little hot oil until golden on both sides.

Bean bake

SERVES 1

A large (400 g/14 oz) can of bean salad or chilli beans

A handful of grated cheese

A packet of salted crisps

1 Heat the beans in a saucepan, then put them in a shallow, flameproof dish.

2 Mix together the cheese and crisps and sprinkle on top.

3 Pop under a pre-heated grill (broiler) for about 5 minutes until the cheese bubbles and the beans are heated through.

Tuna, mayo and sweetcorn

SERVES 1

½ a small (200 g/7 oz) can of tuna in brine, drained

A small (200 g/7 oz) can of sweetcorn (corn), drained

1 tbsp mayonnaise

Pepper

1 Put the tuna and sweetcorn in a bowl.

2 Add the mayonnaise and season with pepper (you won't need salt).

3 Eat as it is out of the bowl or with toast.

Add leftover cooked rice, pasta or potatoes for a filling meal.

Vegetable balti

SERVES 1

1 tbsp vegetable oil

Any vegetables you have to hand – a courgette (zucchini), a piece of cabbage, carrots, broccoli – chopped small

½ a jar of balti curry sauce

A portion of instant noodles

1 Heat the oil and add the vegetables. Stir around for 2–3 minutes.

2 Add the sauce and let it bubble gently while you cook the noodles.

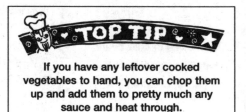

If you have any leftover cooked vegetables to hand, you can chop them up and add them to pretty much any sauce and heat through.

Boiled egg with peanut butter soldiers

SERVES 1

1 egg

2 slices of bread

Peanut butter

1 Boil the egg as described on page 20.

2 Meanwhile, toast the bread and smother in peanut butter.

3 Cut the toast into thin strips and dip into the egg.

Spaghetti surprise

SERVES 1

A large (400 g/14 oz) can of spaghetti in tomato sauce

1 surprise ingredient (my mum uses chopped ham, but a little tuna, chopped mushrooms or sweetcorn would be good)

A small handful of grated cheese

1 slice of bread, cut into small cubes

1 Preheat the grill (broiler). Heat the spaghetti and surprise in a pan.

2 Pour into a flameproof dish and top with the cheese and bread.

3 Grill (broil) for 2 minutes.

TOP TIP

You can use a tin of spaghetti with sausages, or beans with sausages, and top with cheese in the same way.

Tuna and mushroom soup

SERVES 1

1 quantity of mushroom sauce (see page 26)

½ a small (200 g/7 oz) can of tuna in brine, drained

Pepper

Lots of crusty bread

1 Make up the mushroom sauce, but use only 2 tsp of flour.

2 Add the tuna, heat through and season with lots of pepper.

3 Serve with lots of bread.

Mash and mushroom sauce

SERVES 1

1 portion of instant mashed potato

A lump of butter or margarine

½ a medium (300 g/10 oz) can of condensed mushroom soup

1 Make up the potato according to the instructions on the packet. Add the butter or margarine.

2 Heat the soup gently (it will be quite thick) and pour over.

Hot muesli

SERVES 1

Muesli

Milk

1 Fill your favourite cereal bowl with muesli, then pour the muesli into a saucepan.

2 Fill the cereal bowl with milk, then pour that into the pan too.

3 Heat gently, stirring all the time, until the muesli has absorbed most of the milk. Put it back into the cereal bowl. It's like Ready Brek with bits in.

6 After lectures, before the pub

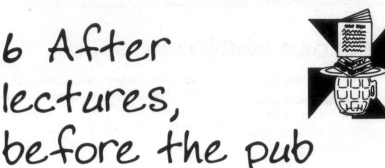

Life's too short to spend too much time in the kitchen, so here's some ideas for keeping body and soul together in under 10 minutes. When you need to feed the team quickly, pasta, salads, omelettes and a few stir-fries will do the trick.

Pasta

Pasta really comes into its own when time is short – it's filling, nutritious and cheap. All it needs is a sauce and that can be made while it's cooking. You could also serve your pasta with a bowl of fresh salad leaves for added nutrition and to jazz up these simple fuel foods.

Use a good handful of dry pasta shapes per person, or a medium (250 g/9 oz) packet for four people. If cooking spaghetti, use half a large (500 g/18 oz) packet (or more for big appetites). The cooking time remains the same, however much you cook – but make sure you have a large enough saucepan.

Long pasta, like spaghetti or tagliatelle, is best for clingy sauces – pesto, carbonara, cheese and onion, Moroccan tomato. Short, stumpy pasta shapes are best for chunky sauces – creamy, leek and bacon, salmon, chickpea (garbanzo), spinach and mushroom.

Chickpea pasta

SERVES 4

4–5 handfuls of pasta shapes

Salt

1 tbsp olive oil

1 garlic clove, crushed

2 large (400 g/14 oz) cans of chickpeas (garbanzos), rinsed and drained

1 tsp chilli powder

2 red (bell) peppers, seeded and chopped

1 Cook the pasta in plenty of boiling salted water according to the packet directions. Drain and return to the pan.

2 Heat the oil in a separate pan and mix in all the other ingredients. Heat through for 5 minutes.

3 Add to the pasta, toss well and serve.

Slacker salmon

SERVES 4

4–5 handfuls of pasta shapes

Salt

A small (200 g/7 oz) can of pink salmon, drained and bones and skin removed

2 tbsp cooked peas or sweetcorn (optional)

4 tbsp mayonnaise

2 tbsp milk

Pepper

1 Cook the pasta in plenty of boiling salted water according to the packet directions. Drain and return to the pan.

2 Put the salmon in a small pan with the peas or sweetcorn, if using, the mayonnaise and milk.

3 Heat through very, very gently, stirring all the time. Mix into the pasta. Season with pepper.

Pesto pasta

SERVES 4

250 g/9 oz long pasta

Salt

2 tbsp pesto sauce

A lump of margarine or 2 tbsp olive oil

Grated Parmesan or Cheddar cheese

1 Cook the pasta in plenty of boiling salted water according to the packet directions. Drain and return to the pan.

2 Add the pesto and margarine or olive oil.

3 Stir it around, then serve with grated Parmesan or Cheddar cheese.

Carbonara pasta

SERVES 4

250 g/9 oz long pasta

Salt

4 rashers (slices) of bacon, chopped (or for veggies 2 handfuls of sliced mushrooms)

1 tbsp oil

4 eggs

2 tbsp grated Parmesan or Cheddar cheese

2 tbsp cream or milk

Pepper

1 Cook the pasta in plenty of boiling salted water according to the packet directions. Drain and return to the pan.

2 Meanwhile, fry the bacon (or mushrooms) in the oil until browned.

3 Beat the eggs, cheese, cream or milk and some pepper in a bowl and stir in the bacon (or mushrooms).

4 Add the carbonara mix to the hot pasta. Stir it around over a gentle heat until lightly scrambled but still creamy.

Cheese and onion pasta

SERVES 4

250 g/9 oz long pasta

Salt

1 onion, chopped

1 tbsp oil

1 tbsp flour

300 ml/½ pt/1¼ cups milk

2 handfuls of grated cheese

1 Cook the pasta in plenty of boiling salted water according to the packet directions. Drain and return to the pan.

2 Meanwhile, fry the onion in the oil until transparent.

3 Add the flour and stir around.

4 Add the milk slowly, stirring as you go. Bring to the boil, stirring all the time until thickened.

5 Add the cheese and stir until melted.

6 Stir into the pasta and serve.

If you're a garlic fan, add a little garlic purée or a crushed garlic clove.

Creamy leek and bacon pasta

SERVES 4

4–5 handfuls of pasta shapes

Salt

2 large leeks, thinly sliced

4 rashers (slices) of bacon, chopped

1 tbsp oil

A small (150 ml/¼ pt/⅔ cup) carton of double (heavy) cream

Pepper

1 Cook the pasta in plenty of boiling salted water according to the packet directions. Drain and return to the pan.

2 Fry the leeks and bacon in the oil until the leeks are soft.

3 Add the cream and season with pepper.

4 Stir into the pasta and serve hot.

TOP TIP

For a lighter sauce, use the same quantity of plain yoghurt instead of the cream.

Moroccan tomato pasta

SERVES 4

250 g/9 oz long pasta

Salt

1 onion, chopped

1 garlic clove, crushed

1 small aubergine (eggplant), topped, tailed and cut into 2.5 cm/1 in cubes

2 tbsp oil

A large (400 g/14 oz) can of chopped tomatoes

1 tbsp raisins or sultanas (golden raisins)

1 tsp ground cumin (optional)

1 Cook the pasta in plenty of boiling salted water according to the packet directions. Drain and return to the pan.

2 Fry the onion, garlic and aubergine in the oil for 5 minutes, stirring.

3 Add the tomatoes, dried fruit and cumin, if using, and heat through. Simmer for 5 minutes until pulpy.

4 Pile the pasta on to warm plates and spoon the sauce over.

Don't have the heat too high when you are frying onions, otherwise they'll burn before they soften.

Spinach and mushroom pasta

SERVES 4

4–5 handfuls of pasta shapes

Salt

1 garlic clove, crushed

4 handfuls of mushrooms, sliced

2 tbsp oil

4 handfuls of fresh spinach, rinsed, de-stalked and chopped

4 large tomatoes, chopped

A small (150 ml/¼ pt/⅔ cup) carton of double (heavy) cream or thick yoghurt

1 Cook the pasta in plenty of boiling salted water according to the packet directions. Drain and return to the pan.

2 Lightly fry the garlic and mushrooms in the oil.

3 Add the spinach and tomatoes to the garlic and mushrooms and keep stirring until the spinach has wilted.

4 Pour in the cream or yoghurt and heat through but do not boil or it will curdle.

5 Add to the pasta, toss and serve.

Frozen spinach can be used instead of fresh.

Salads

Instant and nutritious – all a salad needs is a crisp, fresh base and a good dressing, though almost anything edible can be added. Serve with plenty of crusty bread.

The salad base

This is the veggie bit – any type of lettuce you fancy (washed and torn into pieces), shredded cabbage (red, white or green), sliced cucumber, grated or chopped carrot or other root vegetables, sliced tomato, chopped (bell) peppers, sliced mushrooms, lightly boiled cauliflower or broccoli florets, grated courgette (zucchini).

The salad dressing

This is the oily bit – the classic recipe is one part vinegar or lemon juice to three parts olive oil, mixed and shaken well. Or buy a supermarket brand. This can be altered with splashes of different flavoured oils like walnut or sesame, or soy sauce for an oriental touch.

Always season dressing with salt and pepper. A crushed garlic clove, a dash of chilli or a pinch of dried mixed herbs is good, too.

Salad dressing will keep for up to a week in the fridge.

A dressing based on 1 tbsp of vinegar and 3 tbsp of oil will be enough for a salad to serve 4 people.

Mexican pasta salad

SERVES 4

4 handfuls of pasta shapes,
cooked according to the
packet directions, rinsed
with cold water and drained

A large (425 g/15 oz) can of
red kidney beans, washed
and drained

A small (200 g/7 oz) can of
sweetcorn, drained

1 ripe avocado, peeled and
chopped

Salad dressing (see page
40), made with 1 tsp chilli
powder

Salad base for 4 plates (see
page 40)

1 Mix together the pasta, beans, sweetcorn and avocado.

2 Add the dressing, toss well and spoon on to the salad base.

This is also a good way to use up
leftover pasta.

Hot chicken and bacon salad

SERVES 4

Salad base for 4 plates (see
page 40)

4 tbsp olive oil

4 rashers (slices) of bacon,
chopped

2 chicken breasts, skinned
and cubed

2 tbsp lemon juice

1 Arrange the salad base on four plates.

2 Heat the oil in a frying pan and fry the bacon and chicken for about 7 minutes, stirring occasionally, until both are lightly browned.

3 Add the lemon juice and spoon on to the salads. Serve straight away.

Hot salads can be used as main
courses – serve with lots of good bread.

Eggy salad

SERVES 4

4 eggs

4 tomatoes, sliced

Salad base and dressing for 4 plates (see page 40)

4 tbsp mayonnaise

Oil

4 thick slices of bread (white is best), cubed

1 Boil the eggs for around 8 minutes, then place in cold water until cool enough to shell. Quarter the eggs.

2 Put the eggs and tomatoes on the dressed salad base and spoon the mayonnaise on top.

3 Heat the oil in a small frying pan. Add the bread. Stir over a high heat until the bread is golden and crisp on all sides.

4 Remove the bread from the pan with a draining spoon, drain on kitchen paper (paper towels), then scatter over the salad.

For garlic croûtons (bread cubes), add a crushed clove of garlic to the oil before frying the bread.

Hot and spicy tofu salad

SERVES 4

Salad base for 4 plates (see page 40)

2 tbsp soy sauce

1 tsp chilli powder

1 packet of firm silken tofu, cubed

2 handfuls of mushrooms, sliced

4 tbsp olive oil

A small (200 g/7 oz) can of sweetcorn, drained and rinsed

1 Arrange the salad base on four plates.

2 Mix the soy sauce and chilli powder in a bowl. Add the tofu and leave to marinate for 10 minutes.

3 Fry the mushrooms in the oil, add the tofu, mix together and heat through gently, stirring.

4 Sprinkle the sweetcorn over the salad bases, then put the hot tofu mix on top.

Spinach, bacon and avocado salad

SERVES 4

4 small handfuls of spinach leaves, washed and torn into pieces

Salad base for 4 plates (see page 40)

4 tbsp olive oil

4 rashers (slices) of bacon, chopped (or for veggies 2 handfuls of sliced mushrooms)

1 tbsp lemon juice

2 ripe avocados, peeled and chopped

1 Arrange the spinach on the salad base.

2 Heat the oil in a small frying pan and fry the bacon (or mushrooms) until browned.

3 Add the lemon juice, then pour the entire contents of the pan over the spinach (the hot dressing will wilt the spinach slightly). Scatter the avocado on top and serve straight away.

TOP TIP

An avocado is ripe when you can move the skin around the top with your thumb.

Goats' cheese and grilled pepper salad

SERVES 4

**Salad base and dressing
for 4 plates
(see page 40)**

4 red or yellow (bell) peppers

1 round goats' cheese

1 slice of toast, quartered

1 Arrange the salad base on four plates.

2 Grill (broil) the peppers. Peel if preferred. Slice.

3 Put the slices on top of the salad base and pour the dressing over.

4 Slice the cheese horizontally into four discs and place each one on a quarter of a toast slice. Grill for about 2 minutes or until the cheese browns.

5 Lay them on the peppers and serve.

Oriental noodle salad

SERVES 4

4 handfuls of rice or egg noodles

Salt

4 handfuls of mangetout (snow peas) or frozen peas

4 handfuls of beansprouts

FOR THE DRESSING:

2 tbsp soy sauce

1 tsp chilli powder

Juice of ½ lemon

2 tsp sesame oil

2 tbsp olive oil

1 Cook the rice or noodles in boiling salted water according to the packet directions. Add the mangetout for the last 2 minutes' cooking time.

2 Drain, rinse with cold water and drain again. Return to the pan.

3 Add the beansprouts and stir well.

4 Divide between four plates or bowls.

5 Put all the dressing ingredients in a screw-topped jar and shake well until blended.

6 Pour the dressing over the salad and serve.

Stir-fries

You could live on stir-fries all year. They suit meat eaters and veggies, use cheap ingredients, take minutes to cook and never taste the same twice. There are just a few basic rules to remember:

- Prepare all the ingredients before you start cooking
- Most vegetables will work in a stir-fry – (bell) peppers, carrots, beansprouts, courgettes (zucchini), cabbage, onions, leeks.
- For the meat part, try skinned chicken or turkey breast (or look for prepared stir-fry poultry), pork (shoulder is cheaper than fillet, or you could try de-rinding and cutting up belly rashers into very small pieces) and – if you're budget can run to it – steak. Liver and kidneys are ideal, too.
- Cut all meat into strips (or small pieces for kidneys).
- You need very little meat (the vegetables are the main point of a stir-fry); 2 chicken breasts or 225 g/8 oz of meat will serve 4.
- Cut all the vegetables to the same size so they cook evenly. Aim for chunky batons about 5 cm/2 in long and 5 mm/¼ in thick.
- You will need 6 handfuls of whatever vegetables you use for 4 people – that's the equivalent of 2 courgettes (zucchini), 4 carrots, 2 (bell) peppers and ½ cabbage.
- The flavour of a stir-fry comes from the sauce. There's loads of room to experiment here, but the basic ingredients for 4 are: 4 tbsp soy sauce, 1 tbsp vinegar and 1 tsp of runny honey or sugar.
- Jazz up the sauce with chilli powder, ground ginger, sherry, sesame oil or 1 tbsp prepared sauce such as yellow bean (expensive, but if you use it like this it will last for ages). Mix up all the sauce ingredients in a bowl.
- You must stir-fry on the hob in a wok or deep frying pan.
- Get the wok or frying pan really hot, then add 1 tbsp of cooking oil. Swirl the oil around.
- If you're using meat, add it to the hot oil and cook for 3 minutes. Then add the vegetables and cook for a further 2 minutes. Add the sauce and stir thoroughly for 1 minute more before serving.
- Serve with rice or noodles.

That's all there is to it!

Omelettes

Another made-in-minutes meal that suits most people. Omelettes are best made individually, but you could make one big one using 6–8 eggs and serve a quarter per person. Here's how:

1 Beat 2 eggs in a bowl until they look a bit frothy. Add 2 tbsp water and season well.

2 Choose a topping if you want one – grated cheese, chopped ham, sliced mushrooms, boiled potatoes or simply a pinch of dried mixed herbs all work well.

3 Heat a small knob of margarine or 1 tbsp of oil in a non-stick frying pan.

4 Pour in the egg mixture. Use a wooden spatula to lift and stir the egg until it sets and browns underneath. Keep the heat low so it doesn't burn.

5 Add any topping after 2 minutes' cooking.

6 When brown underneath and almost set, pop it (still in the frying pan) under the grill (broiler) to finish off, if liked.

7 Cut into quarters or fold into three and serve with bread and salad.

More meals in minutes

Here are some more quick ideas.

Tommy eggs

SERVES 4

1 tbsp oil

1 onion, finely chopped

4 rashers (slices) of bacon, chopped (optional)

6 eggs, beaten

4 tomatoes, seeded and chopped

1 Heat the oil in a saucepan and fry the onion and bacon, if using, until the bacon is crisp.

2 Add the eggs and tomatoes and stir around until the eggs are cooked.

This is good served with chips and ketchup (catsup), but toast will do.

Chicken in wine sauce

SERVES 4

1 tbsp oil

4 skinned chicken breasts,
cut into 2 cm/¾ in cubes

2 handfuls of mushrooms,
sliced

1 glass of white wine

A small (150 ml/¼ pt/⅔ cup)
carton of double (heavy)
cream or thick yoghurt

Salt and pepper

TO SERVE:

Rice or pasta

1 Heat the oil in a small frying pan.

2 Add the chicken and stir it around for about 2 minutes until it starts to brown.

3 Add the mushrooms and wine. Cook over a moderate heat for 5 more minutes.

4 Add the cream or yoghurt, heat through and season well. Spoon over rice or pasta.

TOP TIP

This is a luxurious but quick meal when made with chicken breasts. You could use four whole chicken thighs instead, which are much cheaper, but remember they'll take about 20 minutes to cook through.

Thai greens

SERVES 4

2 rashers (slices) of bacon,
chopped small (optional)

1 tbsp oil

Juice of 1 lime

2 tsp sugar

1 tsp chilli powder

2 tbsp soy sauce

2 heads of greens or one
small cabbage, de-stalked
and shredded

2 tbsp water

TO SERVE:

Rice noodles

1 Fry the bacon, if using, in the oil until really crisp. Remove from the pan and put to one side.

2 Put the rest of the ingredients in the pan and stir occasionally for 5 minutes.

3 Add the bacon when the greens are cooked.

4 Serve with rice noodles.

Bacon bits are often cheaper to buy,
although watch out because beautifully
cut 'lardons' will be more expensive.

Malaysian peanut chicken

SERVES 4

3 chicken breasts, skinned
and cut into thin strips

1 tbsp cooking oil

1 green (bell) pepper, cut
into thin strips

2 tbsp peanut butter

2 tbsp soy sauce

½ tsp chilli powder

TO SERVE:

Rice or noodles

1 Fry the chicken gently in the oil until golden
and cooked through.

2 Add all the other ingredients and stir until the
peanut butter melts.

3 Cook for 5 minutes more, then serve with
rice or noodles.

TOP TIP

Chicken or turkey goujons are also ideal
for this dish.

Spinach and bean bhaji

SERVES 4

4 tbsp margarine

2 onions, peeled and sliced into thin rings

1 garlic clove, crushed

1 tsp garam masala or ground cumin

1 tsp ground ginger or chilli powder

2 large (425 g/15 oz) cans of red kidney beans, drained and rinsed

Lots and lots of spinach – never underestimate how much spinach cooks down – for this you need at least 900 g/2 lb

TO SERVE:

Plain yoghurt and naan bread or rice

1 Melt the margarine in a large pan.

2 Fry the onions until golden, then add the garlic and spices. Cook for 1 minute more.

3 Add the beans and spinach. Keep the spinach moving with a wooden spoon – it'll soon wilt down.

4 Serve with yoghurt and naan bread or rice.

Line the grill (broiler) pan with foil whenever you use it to save those 'grilled-on grease' washing-up problems.

7 Light meals and snacks

Not exactly starving, but definitely in need of nourishment? Nip into the kitchen and whip up a snack. Here's a few quick and easy ideas that should fire up your imagination.

Veggie sticks and avocado dip

SERVES 1–2

Sticks cut from peeled carrots, cucumber, celery and anything else you fancy

FOR THE DIP:

1 ripe avocado, mashed

A small (150 ml/¼ pt/⅔ cup) carton of plain yoghurt

½ tsp chilli powder

2 tomatoes and/or a piece of cucumber, finely chopped (optional)

Salt and pepper

1 Arrange the vegetable sticks in a bowl or on a plate.

2 Mix together all the dip ingredients and season well.

If you have to leave the dip around for a while before eating, put the avocado stone in to stop the flesh going brown, or sprinkle with lemon juice.

BLT

SERVES 1

2 or 3 rashers (slices) of
bacon

2 slices of bread

Lots of mayonnaise

1 tomato, sliced

A handful of lettuce

This is the classic American sandwich – bacon, lettuce and tomato.

1 Grill (broil) the bacon until really crisp.

2 Toast the bread and spread generously with mayonnaise.

3 Pile the tomato and lettuce on to one slice of toast, top with the bacon, then the remaining slice of toast.

Try substituting fish fingers for the bacon for an English version.

BCT

SERVES 1

2 rashers (slices) of bacon

2 slices of bread

Slices of cheese

1 tomato, sliced

A variation on the classic BLT, with bacon, cheese and tomato.

1 Grill (broil) the bacon and put to one side.

2 Toast the bread and top with the slices of cheese. Grill the cheese until it bubbles.

3 Top with the tomato slices and bacon, then the remaining slice of toast.

Pitta pizza

SERVES 1

1 large pitta bread

Tomato purée (paste) or ketchup (catsup)

Sliced mushrooms or tomatoes (optional)

A piece of cheese, sliced or grated

1 Grill (broil) one side of the bread. Spread tomato purée on the ungrilled side.

2 Top with the mushrooms or tomato, if using, and the cheese.

3 Grill again until the cheese melts.

You can sprinkle the top with extra herbs, if you like.

Mayo eggs

SERVES 1

A lump of margarine

2 eggs

1 tbsp milk

2 tsp mayonnaise

Salt and pepper

2 slices of toast

1 Melt the margarine in a saucepan on the lowest possible heat.

2 Add the eggs and beat them with a wooden spoon.

3 Pour in the milk and keep stirring all the time.

4 Add the mayonnaise and season well. Be patient. Don't turn the heat up or give up the stirring.

5 When the eggs begin to set, serve on toast.

Saucy mushrooms

SERVES 4

A lump of margarine

**4 large handfuls of
mushrooms, sliced**

1 tsp dried mixed herbs

2 wine glasses of milk

**1 tsp cornstarch (cornflour),
mixed with 1 tbsp water**

TO SERVE:

Toast

1 Melt the margarine in a saucepan and fry the mushrooms gently.

2 Add the herbs and milk and cook until the mushrooms start to absorb the milk.

3 Add the blended cornstarch and cook, stirring all the time, until the sauce thickens. Simmer for 1 minute. Serve with toast.

Garlic bread

SERVES 4

1 French stick

4 tbsp soft margarine

2 garlic cloves, crushed

1 tsp dried mixed herbs

1 Preheat the oven to 190°C/375°F/gas 5/fan oven 170°C.

2 Cut the loaf in half (so it will fit into the oven), then make cuts from the top almost to the bottom (the slices should still just be joined to the loaf at the bottom), about 5 cm/2 in apart.

3 In a bowl, mash together the margarine, garlic and herbs. Spread the mixture into the cuts in the loaf.

4 Wrap each half of the loaf in foil and cook in the oven for 15 minutes.

Soups

There are two types of soup – creamy and clear. Creamy ones are made in the same way as the white sauce recipe on page 26, using flour and milk. Clear ones have water and flavouring. You'll need around 900 ml/1½ pts/ 3¾ cups of liquid to make soup for 4. If in doubt, fill a bowl with milk or water and use that as a measuring guide.

Serve soup with bread and salad for a more substantial meal.

French onion soup

SERVES 4

2 tbsp margarine

4 small onions, cut into very thin rings

900 ml/1½ pts/3¾ cups water

2 beef stock cubes

2 slices of bread, toasted and quartered (or 8 thin slices of French stick, toasted)

A handful of grated cheese

1 Melt the margarine in a large saucepan and fry the onion rings until soft.

2 Add the water and bring to the boil.

3 Crumble in the stock cubes and simmer gently for 5 minutes.

4 Top the toast quarters with the cheese and grill (broil) until melted. Float two in each bowl of soup.

If you buy a strongly flavoured cheese, you won't need to use so much.

Noodle soup

SERVES 4

900 ml/1½ pts/3¾ cups water

2 vegetable stock cubes

4 blocks of noodles

1 tsp chilli powder

2 tbsp soy sauce

Anything else you have to hand – a handful of frozen peas, a small can of sweetcorn (corn), drained; chopped cooked meat; finely chopped veg like broccoli or courgette (zucchini), grated carrot

1 Boil the water in a saucepan, crumble in the stock cubes and stir until dissolved.

2 Add the noodles, the chilli powder and soy sauce. Stir in your extra ingredients.

3 Boil gently for 3 minutes or follow the instructions on the noodle packet.

This is so easy and quick but tastes surprisingly good!

Bread and bean soup

SERVES 4

1 tbsp oil

2 leeks, thinly sliced

4 large tomatoes, sliced, or a small (200 g/7 oz) can of chopped tomatoes

1 garlic clove, chopped

1 vegetable stock cube

900 ml/1½ pts/3¾ cups water

A large (425 g/15 oz) can of butter (lima) beans, drained and rinsed

4 slices of white bread, cubed

1 tsp vinegar

1 Heat the oil in a saucepan and fry the leeks over a low heat for 5 minutes.

2 Add the tomatoes and garlic and cook for a further 5 minutes.

3 Crumble in the stock cube and add the water. Bring to the boil, then simmer gently while you add the beans and bread.

4 Switch off the heat and allow the soup to stand for 2 minutes before adding the vinegar. Serve straight away.

TOP TIP

If you burn food, don't panic. A splash of milk can take away the burnt taste of a sauce (be careful not to scrape the blackened base of the pan into the sauce) and a burnt topping can be scraped off with a flat-bladed knife.

8 Mum, I miss you - a bit of home cooking

No one makes it quite like mum, right? Well, now you can have a good try. These recipes take longer to cook, so a bit of planning is required, but they are very easy and will delight your housemates – and mum if she comes to visit. Serve with salad or cooked vegetables.

Most of these recipes reheat well so, if you know you'll be in, make double to save time tomorrow. But do wait until the cooked food is completely cold before putting it in the fridge. Keep it covered and away from raw food. Reheat in a hot oven until piping hot all through – never just warm.

Baked potatoes

SERVES 4

One of the world's best comfort foods – and which results in the minimum of washing up! Bake 4 potatoes following the instructions on page 22. Halve, then mash a lump of margarine into each one. Season with salt and pepper, then top with one of the following:

Cheese: 4 handfuls of grated cheese. Pile on top of the potatoes and grill (broil) briefly.

Tuna: Mix a drained small (150 g/5 oz) can of tuna and a small (200 g/7 oz) can of sweetcorn with lots of mayonnaise. Alternatively, mix the tuna into a tub of coleslaw. Pile on to the potatoes.

Chilli bean: Gently simmer a large (400 g/14 oz) can of tomatoes, a large (425 g/15 oz) can of red kidney beans in chilli sauce and 2 handfuls of sliced mushrooms in a saucepan for 10 minutes. Spoon on to the potatoes and sprinkle a little grated cheese over the top.

Canny ideas: Try heating a large (425 g/15 oz) can of ratatouille or baked beans with sausages or vegetable curry or condensed mushroom soup. Spoon over the potatoes and serve.

Shepherd's pie

SERVES 4

1 large onion, chopped

750 g/1¾ lb minced (ground)
lamb or beef

2 carrots, grated

A small (200 g/7 oz) can of
chopped tomatoes

2 large potatoes, chopped

A lump of margarine

1 tbsp milk

Salt and pepper

1 Dry-fry the onion with the meat in a saucepan, stirring, until the meat is browned and crumbly.

2 Add the carrots and tomatoes and simmer for 20 minutes.

3 Meanwhile, boil the potatoes in plenty of salted water until tender, then mash with the margarine, the milk and salt and pepper to taste.

4 Pour the meat mixture into a flameproof dish and top with the potato. Grill (broil) for 5 minutes or until the potato is turning brown.

As an alternative you can replace the tomatoes with an equivalent quantity of gravy made with gravy granules.

Saunders pie

This is a cheat's version of Shepherd's Pie.

SERVES 4

A large (400 g/14 oz) can of baked beans

A medium (350 g/12 oz) can of corned beef

Mashed potato (see page 21)

1 Put the beans in a saucepan.

2 Mash the corned beef and add to the beans.

3 Heat the beans and corned beef through, then pour into a flameproof dish and top with the potato. Grill (broil) for 5 minutes or until the potato is turning brown.

TOP TIP

If you are in a real hurry, you could use instant mashed potato – add a splash of milk and some butter for extra flavour.

Veggie shepherd's pie

SERVES 4

1 tbsp oil

1 large onion, chopped

1 garlic clove, crushed

A large (400 g/14 oz) can of ratatouille

A large (425 g/15 oz) can of pulses (cooked dried beans), drained and rinsed

2 carrots, grated

2 large potatoes, chopped

A lump of margarine

A handful of grated cheese

1–2 tbsp milk

Salt and pepper

1 Heat the oil in a large saucepan and fry the onion until translucent.

2 Add the garlic, ratatouille, pulses and carrots. Simmer for 5 minutes.

3 Meanwhile, boil the potatoes in salted water until tender, then mash them with the margarine, cheese and milk.

4 Season the vegetable mixture well, then pour into a flameproof dish and top with the potato.

5 Grill (broil) for 5 minutes or until the potato is turning brown.

TOP TIP

Pulses are an important part of a vegetarian diet instead of meat. Cooking them from their dried state is cheap but time consuming – they need to be soaked overnight, then boiled rapidly for 10 minutes to destroy toxins, before simmering until tender. Only red lentils are safe to cook without soaking. Do not add salt. It's much less trouble to buy them ready cooked in cans. Drain and rinse before using.

Quick fish pie

SERVES 4

450 g/1 lb of cheap white fish such as coley, hoki or whiting

600 ml/1 pt/2½ cups milk

1 leek, sliced, or one red (bell) pepper, seeded and chopped (optional)

2 large potatoes, diced

3 tbsp margarine

A splash of milk

Salt and pepper

1 tbsp flour

A 2.5 cm/1 in thick slab of cheese, chopped

1 Put the fish in a saucepan. Cover with the milk, add the leek or pepper, if using, and poach on a low heat for 10 minutes until the fish flakes easily when pushed with a fork.

2 Meanwhile, cook the potatoes in boiling salted water until tender.

3 Drain and mash the potatoes with 1 tbsp of the margarine, a splash of milk and salt and pepper.

4 Heat the remaining margarine and stir in the flour. Lift the cooked fish and vegetables from the milk and place in a flameproof dish. Break up the fish with a fork and discard the skin and any bones.

5 Pour the milk from the fish into the flour mixture. Stir constantly over a moderate heat until thickened. Add the cheese. Pour the sauce on to the fish and top with the mashed potato.

6 Pop under the grill (broiler) for 5 minutes or until the potato is turning brown.

TOP TIP

Never re-freeze food. A lot of fish has been frozen on its way to the shop, so don't store it in the freezer for a later date – use it as quickly as possible.

Cauliflower cheese

SERVES 4

1 cauliflower, cut into florets

4 handfuls of pasta shapes

1 tbsp oil

1 tbsp flour

600 ml/1 pt/2½ cups milk

2 handfuls of grated hard cheese such as Cheddar

1 tbsp grated Parmesan cheese (optional)

1 Put the cauliflower and pasta in a saucepan of boiling water and boil for about 8 minutes until cooked.

2 Heat the oil in a small saucepan, add the flour and stir well.

3 Add the milk slowly to the flour mixture with half the cheese.

4 Drain the pasta and cauliflower, then tip into a flameproof dish.

5 Pour on the sauce and top with the remaining cheese, plus the Parmesan, if using.

6 Grill (broil) until the cheese starts bubbling.

Potato and bacon pie

SERVES 4

4 large potatoes, scrubbed and sliced

6 rashers (slices) of bacon

Oil

4 large tomatoes, sliced

A 5 cm/2 in piece of Cheddar cheese, thinly sliced

1 Boil the potato slices in salted water for about 5–10 minutes until cooked.

2 Grill (broil) the bacon until crisp, then chop into small pieces.

3 Oil a heatproof dish and fill with alternate layers of potato, bacon, tomato slices and cheese. Finish with a layer of cheese.

4 Bake in a preheated oven at 190°C/375°F/gas 5/fan oven 170°C for 20 minutes or until hot through, bubbling and golden.

TOP TIP

Once you've opened a packet of cheese, wrap the remainder in foil to stop it from going hard.

Cheap chilli

SERVES 4

1 tbsp oil

1 large onion, chopped

450 g/1 lb minced (ground) beef

A large (400 g/14 oz) can of chopped tomatoes

A large (400 g/14 oz) can of red kidney beans, drained and rinsed

1 tsp chilli powder (or less or more to taste)

4 large handfuls of rice

4 handfuls of chopped lettuce

2 tomatoes, chopped

1 Heat the oil in saucepan and fry the onion and mince, stirring, until the meat is browned and crumbly.

2 Add the tomatoes, beans and chilli powder.

3 Simmer gently for about 30 minutes until cooked through and thick.

4 Cook the rice in boiling salted water until tender. Drain and divide into bowls or deep plates. Pour the chilli mixture over and top with chopped lettuce and tomatoes.

TOP TIP

When browning mince, pour off as much fat as you can into a bowl so it's not too greasy. Allow the fat to set, then throw it away – or put it out for the birds. Don't pour it straight down the sink or it could solidify and block the drain.

Spaghetti bolognese

SERVES 4

1 tbsp oil

1 garlic clove, crushed

1 onion, chopped

450 g/1 lb minced (ground) beef

A large (400 g/14 oz) can of chopped tomatoes

1 tsp dried mixed herbs

250 g/9 oz spaghetti

4 tbsp grated Cheddar or Parmesan cheese

1 Heat the oil in a saucepan and brown the garlic and onion.

2 Add the meat and fry, stirring, until browned and crumbly.

3 Add the tomatoes and herbs and simmer for 20 minutes.

4 Cook the spaghetti in plenty of boiling salted water according to the packet directions. Drain.

5 Pile the spaghetti on to plates, top with the meat and sprinkle the cheese on top.

Spaghetti lentilese

SERVES 4

Make as for Spaghetti Bolognese, but substitute the meat with four handfuls of red lentils (they don't need browning).

Fruity bean stew

SERVES 4

1 tbsp oil

1 onion, chopped

1 garlic clove, chopped

1 red and 1 green (bell) pepper, seeded and chopped

2 carrots, peeled and sliced

2 large (425 g/15 oz) cans of pulses (e.g. black-eyed beans), drained and rinsed

A large (400 g/14 oz) can of chopped tomatoes

1 orange, peeled and chopped

2 handfuls of raisins or sultanas (golden raisins)

4 tbsp orange juice

1 tsp dried mixed herbs

A small (snack-size) bag of sunflower seeds or unsalted peanuts (optional)

TO SERVE:

Potatoes or rice

1 Heat the oil in a large saucepan and lightly fry the onion and garlic.

2 Add all the other ingredients except the sunflower seeds or nuts, if using.

3 Simmer gently for 20 minutes.

4 Top with the sunflower seeds or nuts, if using, and serve with potatoes or rice.

TOP TIP

To chop an onion, the least painful way is to cut the top off the onion, then cut it in half from top to bottom. Lay each half cut-side down on the chopping board. Peel off the brown skin and bin it. Hold on to the root base and makes cuts from top to root. Then cut across horizontally into little squares. Discard the root.

Sausage casserole

SERVES 4

8 large or 12 medium sausages (meat or veggie)

1 onion, chopped

4 tomatoes, chopped

2 small eating (dessert) apples (Cox's have the best flavour), cored and chopped

Apple juice or cider (or half and half)

1 tsp cornflour (cornstarch)

TO SERVE:

Mashed potato

1 Dry-fry the sausages in a frying pan until lightly browned all over.

2 Place the onion, tomatoes and apples in a casserole dish (Dutch oven) and lay the sausages on top.

3 Pour in enough apple juice or cider to half cover the sausages.

4 Mix the cornflour with 1 tbsp of the juice or cider and pour over the casserole. Cover (with foil if you don't have a lid).

5 Bake in a preheated oven at 190°C/ 375°F/gas 5/fan oven 170°C for 30 minutes. Remove the cover and cook for 10 minutes more. Serve with mashed potato.

TOP TIP

You get what you pay for when buying sausages, so avoid the cheapest if you can. They'll contain a lot of bread – and you probably wouldn't want to know what else.

Liver and bacon

SERVES 4

1 tbsp oil

2 onions, sliced

4 rashers (slices) of bacon

450 g/1 lb pigs' or lambs' liver

1 beef or vegetable stock cube

300 ml/½ pt/1¼ cups water

1 tsp cornflour (cornstarch), mixed with 1 tbsp water

TO SERVE:

Rice or mashed potato

1 Heat the oil in a large frying pan and brown the onions.

2 Add the bacon and liver and crumble in the stock cube. Brown gently, then pour in the water and stir in the cornflour mix.

3 Cook over a low heat for 15 minutes. Serve with rice or mashed potato.

TOP TIP

If you like your bacon really crispy, you can grill (broil) it separately.

Cheesy layer

SERVES 4

1 tbsp oil

4 carrots, sliced

4 large potatoes, peeled and thinly sliced

1 small cabbage, de-stalked and sliced

A handful of mushrooms, sliced

4 handfuls of green beans, frozen or fresh

2 handfuls of grated cheese

2 eggs

300 ml/½ pt/1¼ cups milk

Salt and pepper

1 Swirl the oil around in a large heatproof dish.

2 Layer in the vegetables and cheese, ending with cheese.

3 Beat the eggs into the milk and season well.

4 Pour over the vegetables and cheese and bake in a preheated oven at 190°C/ 375°F/gas 5/fan oven 170°C for 1 hour.

If you have a freezer, a couple of bags of frozen veg – beans, peas, corn or whatever you like – are useful for lots of dishes. And healthy too!

Fish chowder

SERVES 4

225 g/8 oz smoked fish (e.g. haddock or cod)

2 tbsp oil

1 tbsp flour

900 ml/1½ pts/3¾ cups milk

4 potatoes, diced

A selection of vegetables – sliced carrots, sliced courgettes (zucchini), shredded cabbage, peas, chopped tomatoes, watercress, spinach

4 handfuls of grated cheese

TO SERVE:

Crusty bread

1 Skin the fish: put it skin-side down on a chopping board. Hold one end firmly and work a sharp knife between the flesh and skin, gradually pushing the flesh back. Discard the skin. Cut the fish into pieces.

2 Heat the oil in a large saucepan.

3 Stir in the flour and gradually blend in the milk and bring gently to a simmer, stirring until smooth.

4 Add the fish, potatoes and other vegetables.

5 Return to a simmer for about 15 minutes, stirring gently occasionally, until the fish and vegetables are cooked.

6 Sprinkle the cheese over and serve with lots of bread.

9 Showing off

Now you feel completely at home in your kitchen, let's get a little more sophisticated because, however hectic life becomes, there will be times when you want to sit down with your mates and have a proper meal.

Chicken in a pot

SERVES 4

1.5 kg/3 lb oven-ready chicken (completely thawed if frozen)

1 onion, peeled and quartered

1 lemon, cut into chunks

4 celery sticks, sliced

2 red or yellow (bell) peppers, seeded and sliced

A small handful of stoned (pitted) olives, rinsed (optional)

Salt and pepper

3 garlic cloves, crushed

1 tsp dried mixed herbs

½ a bottle of dry white wine

TO SERVE:

Potatoes and a green vegetable

1 Remove the giblets from the chicken cavity (if present), then rinse the chicken inside and out and dry with kitchen paper (paper towels).

2 Put the onion and half the lemon chunks in the body cavity.

3 Put the celery, peppers, olives, if using, and remaining lemon in a casserole dish (Dutch oven). Place the chicken on top, season with salt and pepper and sprinkle the garlic and herbs over. Pour the wine over the top and cover with a lid or foil.

4 Cook in a preheated oven at 190°C/375°F/gas 5/fan oven 170°C for 1 hour 20 minutes. Remove the cover and cook for a further 20 minutes.

5 Serve with potatoes and a green vegetable.

Cheese and aubergine pie

SERVES 4

2 aubergines (eggplants)

Oil

1 onion, chopped

A large (400 g/14 oz) can of chopped tomatoes

1 tsp dried mixed herbs

4 handfuls of grated Cheddar cheese

TO SERVE:

Tagliatelle

1 Top and tail the aubergines, then slice into discs slightly thicker than a pound coin (5 mm) and prepare as described below (if you have time).

2 Lightly oil a heatproof casserole dish (Dutch oven).

3 Fry the onion in 1 tbsp of oil until transparent.

4 Add the tomatoes and herbs and cook for 5 minutes.

5 Spread a thin layer of the tomato sauce on the bottom of the casserole dish. Cover with a layer of aubergine slices. Sprinkle some of the cheese on top.

6 Continue the layers until you run out of ingredients or the dish is full. Finish with a layer of cheese.

7 Bake in a preheated oven at 200°C/400°F/gas 6/fan oven 180°C for 30 minutes or until the aubergines are tender when a knife is pushed down in the centre of the dish. Serve with tagliatelle.

TOP TIP

Aubergines can be bitter, but salting and draining them, though not essential, will improve the taste. Slice or cube them and place in a colander over a bowl or the sink. Sprinkle with salt and leave to stand for 20–30 minutes. Rinse thoroughly, then cook as required.

Thai vegetable curry

SERVES 4

2 aubergines (eggplants), cut
into 2 cm/¾ in cubes

A large (400 g/14 oz) can of
coconut milk

2 tbsp oil

1 onion, chopped

2 garlic cloves, chopped

2 tbsp Thai red or green
curry paste

4 courgettes (zucchini), cut
into thick chunks

1 red (bell) pepper, seeded
and sliced

Finely grated rind and juice
of 1 lime or lemon

1 tsp sugar

2 tbsp soy sauce

A few fresh coriander
(cilantro) leaves (optional)

TO SERVE:

Noodles

1 Salt and drain the aubergines as on page 73 (if you have time).

2 Open the coconut milk, then leave it in the fridge for at least an hour so the cream can rise to the top – don't stir it!

3 Heat the oil in a saucepan and lightly fry the onion and garlic.

4 Add the curry paste and fry until it starts to separate, then add the courgettes and sliced pepper.

5 Skim off 6 tbsp of the thick coconut cream and add to the pan. Simmer gently for 10 minutes.

6 Stir in the lime or lemon rind and juice, the sugar and soy sauce. Garnish with coriander leaves, if liked, and serve with noodles.

Cook-in sauces are a useful standby but the cheaper they are, the more additives they are likely to contain.

Stuffed trout

SERVES 4

4 tbsp margarine, melted

4 tbsp lemon juice

4 mushrooms, finely chopped

2 slices of bread, crusts removed, finely chopped

Salt and pepper

4 fresh, cleaned rainbow trout

TO SERVE:

Potatoes and a green vegetable

1 In a small bowl, mix together half the margarine, half the lemon juice, the mushrooms and bread. Season with salt and pepper.

2 Rinse the fish and wipe with kitchen paper (paper towels).

3 Stuff the mushroom mixture into the cavities.

4 Place in a heatproof dish, pour the remaining margarine and lemon juice over and cover with foil or a lid.

5 Cook in a preheated oven at 190°C/375°F/ gas 5/fan oven 170°C for 30 minutes.

6 Serve with potatoes and a green vegetable.

For a cheaper dish, use mackerel instead of rainbow trout.

Vegetable goulash

SERVES 4

1 tbsp oil

1 onion, chopped

1 garlic clove, crushed

2 handfuls of broccoli florets

1 red (bell) pepper, seeded
and sliced

1 green pepper, seeded and
sliced

4 courgettes (zucchini),
thickly sliced

½ Savoy cabbage,
de-stalked and sliced

2 large (400 g/14 oz) cans of
tomatoes

2 tbsp sherry

A small (150 ml/¼ pt/⅔ cup)
carton of soured (dairy sour)
cream to garnish

TO SERVE:

Rice

1 Heat the oil in a large saucepan and fry the
onion until transparent.

2 Add the garlic, cook briefly, then add all the
other vegetables and the tomatoes. Add the
sherry and bring to the boil.

3 Turn down the heat and simmer gently for
15 minutes until the vegetables are cooked
but not soggy.

4 Serve with rice and dollop the soured cream
on top.

TOP TIP

Booze adds lots of flavour to food and
needn't be expensive – any old rubbish
will do. It's worth investing in a bottle of
cheap British sherry just to pep up
dishes. Don't drink it, even when
desperate – the hangover will be horrible!

Stuffed chicken breasts

SERVES 4

4 boneless chicken breasts

½ a small (175 g/6 oz) carton of cream cheese, or 1 garlic and herb cheese such as Boursin (about 85 g/3½ oz)

1 red (bell) pepper, seeded and thinly sliced

2 glasses of white wine

TO SERVE:

French Potatoes (see page 78) and broccoli

1 Place one chicken breast on a chopping board with the thickest part facing you. With a sharp knife, make a small pocket in the side (imagine it's a pitta bread and you're making a doner kebab).

2 Spread a layer of the cheese along the bottom of the pocket and top with a few strips of pepper. Repeat for each chicken breast, reserving about a third of the cheese for the sauce.

3 Carefully place each piece of chicken in a casserole dish (Dutch oven), closing the 'pockets' as you go. Place any remaining pepper strips in the dish as well.

4 Pour the wine over, cover and bake in a preheated oven at 200°C/400°F/gas 6/fan oven 180°C for 30 minutes until the chicken is cooked through.

5 Put the chicken pieces on plates and stir the remaining cheese into the dish so it melts with the wine to form a sauce. Spoon over the chicken.

6 Serve with French Potatoes and broccoli.

French potatoes

SERVES 4

1 tbsp oil

4 large potatoes, thinly sliced

2 large onions, sliced into thin rings

A lump of margarine

Salt and pepper

1 mugful of milk

1 Swirl the oil around in an ovenproof dish.

2 Put a layer of potatoes, then a layer of onion rings, then a few flakes of margarine into the dish and season with salt and pepper. Repeat until all the ingredients are used.

3 Pour the milk over.

4 Bake in a preheated oven at 200°C/400°F/gas 6/fan oven 180°C for 1¼ hours.

If serving with Stuffed Chicken Breasts (see page 77), get this dish in the oven before you prepare the chicken.

Home-made pizza

SERVES 4

2 tsp salt

1 tsp sugar

1 sachet of easy-blend dried yeast

3 mugfuls of flour, preferably strong (bread) flour, but plain (all-purpose) will do

2 tbsp olive oil, plus extra for greasing

About 450 ml/¾ pt/2 cups warm (not hot) water

4 tbsp tomato purée (paste)

4 handfuls of sliced mushrooms

4 handfuls of grated cheese

1 tsp dried mixed herbs

TO SERVE:

Salad

1 Put the salt, sugar, yeast and flour in a bowl and mix with a wooden spoon.

2 Make a well in the centre, pour in the oil and mix with enough of the warm water until the mixture forms a dough that comes away from the side of the bowl.

3 Place on a floured surface and knead well for a few minutes. Really bash it around (pretend it's someone you hate!).

4 Put the dough in an oiled plastic bag and leave for 30 minutes to rise.

5 Knead the dough for a minute more (it will return to its unrisen size), then divide in half.

6 Flatten each half into a round and place on oiled baking sheets.

7 Spread tomato purée over each one and top with the mushrooms, then the cheese and herbs.

8 Bake in a preheated oven at 230°C/ 450°F/gas 8/fan oven 210°C for 15 minutes or until golden and bubbling. Cut up using scissors and serve with salad.

TOP TIP

If you don't want to make your own base, buy a ready-made one and brush with olive oil before using (they tend to be a bit dry).

Vegetable puff pie

SERVES 4

Flour for dusting

A slab of puff pastry (paste) (about 250 g/9 oz), thawed if frozen

1 tbsp oil, plus extra for greasing

2 leeks, thinly sliced

1 red (bell) pepper, seeded and chopped small

4 handfuls of sliced mushrooms

2 handfuls of cooked rice (see page 21), cooled

2 tbsp soy sauce

1 tsp dried mixed herbs

1 egg, beaten

TO SERVE:

Salad

1 Sprinkle some flour on a (clean!) work surface or large chopping board.

2 Roll out the pastry until it's about 30 cm/ 12 in square.

3 Heat the oil in a pan and lightly fry the leeks, chopped pepper and mushrooms.

4 Add the rice, soy sauce and herbs.

5 Rub some oil on a baking (cookie) sheet. Place the pastry on it and pile the vegetable mixture on to one half.

6 Spread a little of the beaten egg around the edge of the pastry. Fold over the remaining pastry so it looks like a big Cornish pasty and pinch the edges together well to seal.

7 Brush more egg on the top and make a small slit in the top with a knife (this allows steam to escape).

8 Bake in a preheated oven at 220°C/ 425°F/gas 7/fan oven 200°C for 15–20 minutes until risen and golden brown. Serve with salad.

If you don't have a rolling pin, use a clean milk or wine bottle and rub some flour on to it.

Instead of a pastry brush, use your finger to spread the egg around the edge of the pastry.

Cheese fondue

SERVES 4

½ a bottle of white wine

1 garlic clove, crushed

1 tbsp cornflour (cornstarch)

450 g/1 lb Cheddar, Emmental or Gruyère (Swiss) cheese, grated

Salt and pepper

1 French stick, cut into 1 cm/½ in cubes

Sticks of fresh vegetables such as carrots and celery

1 Pour the wine into a heavy-based saucepan and add the garlic. Heat until almost boiling. Spoon out the garlic and discard.

2 Mix the cornflour with the cheese and stir into the wine. Keep stirring over a gentle heat until it's all melted and the mixture is thick and creamy.

3 Season well and serve in the pan with bread, the vegetables and forks for dipping.

TOP TIP

The first person to drop their bread into the fondue has to down their drink/buy a round/wash up.

Lasagne

SERVES 4

1 tbsp oil, plus extra for greasing

1 onion, chopped

2 garlic cloves, crushed

1 carrot, grated

350 g/12 oz minced (ground) beef

2 glasses of red wine (optional)

150 ml/¼ pt/⅔ cup milk

A large (400 g/14 oz) can of chopped tomatoes

1 tbsp tomato purée (paste)

1 tsp dried mixed herbs

2 packets of cheese sauce mix

8–10 sheets of no-need-to-precook lasagne

2 handfuls of grated cheese

TO SERVE:

Salad

1 Heat the oil in a large saucepan. Add the onion, garlic and carrot and cook until they start to colour.

2 Add the meat and stir until brown and crumbly.

3 Pour in the wine, if using, and the milk and boil rapidly until most of the liquid has evaporated.

4 Stir in the tomatoes, tomato purée and herbs. Simmer over a low heat for 20–30 minutes.

5 Make up the cheese sauce according to the packet directions.

6 Oil an ovenproof dish. Cover the bottom with a thin layer of meat sauce. Cover with a layer of lasagne. Do another layer of meat sauce, then pasta, then some cheese sauce. Repeat the layers until all the ingredients are used, finishing with a layer of cheese sauce.

7 Sprinkle the grated cheese over and bake in a preheated oven at 190ºC/375ºF/gas 5/fan oven 170ºC for 45 minutes or until the lasagne feels soft when a knife is pushed down through the centre.

8 Serve with salad.

Vegetable lasagne

SERVES 4

2 tbsp oil, plus extra for
greasing

2 garlic cloves, chopped

1 aubergine (eggplant),
cubed

2 leeks, sliced

8 handfuls of spinach, rinsed
and torn into pieces

1 red (bell) pepper, seeded
and chopped

4 tomatoes, chopped

2 small (150 ml/¼ pt/⅔ cup)
cartons of plain yoghurt

2 packets of cheese
sauce mix

8–10 sheets of no-need-to-
precook lasagne

2 handfuls of grated cheese

TO SERVE:

Salad

1 Heat the oil in a saucepan and lightly fry all the vegetables and the tomatoes for 5 minutes.

2 Mix in the yoghurt.

3 Make up the cheese sauce according to the packet directions.

4 Oil an ovenproof dish. Cover the bottom with a layer of the vegetable mix, then pour over some cheese sauce and cover with lasagne sheets. Repeat the layering process, ending with pasta, then cheese sauce.

5 Sprinkle the grated cheese over.

6 Bake in a preheated oven at 180°C/350°F/gas 4/fan oven 160°C for 45 minutes until cooked through. Serve with salad.

TOP TIP

Parmesan is ideal for sprinkling on
the top, but you can use any strong
hard cheese.

Pork casserole

SERVES 4

2 tbsp oil

450 g/1 lb lean cubed pork

2 apples, cored and chopped

1 red (bell) pepper, seeded and chopped

1 leek, chopped

1 tbsp flour

Apple juice

Salt and pepper

TO SERVE:

Baked potatoes (see page 22) and spring (collard) greens

1 Heat the oil in a large frying pan. Add the meat and brown on all sides.

2 Add the apples, chopped pepper and leek.

3 Sprinkle the flour over and stir well.

4 Turn into a heatproof dish and pour in enough apple juice to just cover the meat. Season with salt and pepper and stir well.

5 Cook in a preheated oven at 160°C/325°F/gas 3/fan oven 145°C for at least 1½ hours until tender.

6 Serve with baked potatoes and spring greens.

10 Sweet treats

Never trust someone who says they don't have a sweet tooth. They must be a control freak. Everyone reaches a stage in their life when they need a pudding – don't they?

Lemon ice-cream

SERVES 4

A large (600 ml/1 pt/2½ cup) carton of plain yoghurt

450 g/1 lb lemon curd

Finely grated rind of 1 lemon (optional)

1 You'll need a large plastic box with a lid (an old plastic ice-cream container is ideal).

2 Tip all the ingredients into the box and mix really well.

3 Put in the freezer or freezing compartment of the fridge for at least 2 hours (it'll keep for about a month) and take out 15 minutes before you want to eat it.

Mars bar sauce

SERVES 4

3 Mars bars

3 tbsp milk or cream

3 tbsp sherry or brandy

Vanilla ice-cream

1 Chop the Mars bars into small chunks and put in a heatproof bowl with the milk or cream and the alcohol.

2 Put the bowl over a saucepan of gently simmering water and stir gently until the Mars bars have melted.

3 Pour over the ice-cream and enjoy.

Fruit salad brûlée

SERVES 4

Mixed fresh fruit such as 1 banana, 1 apple, 1 orange

A large (425 g/15 oz) can of peach slices in fruit juice

A large (600 ml/1 pint/ 2½ cup) carton of fromage frais, crème frâiche or thick plain yoghurt

A small (150 ml/¼ pt/⅔ cup) carton of extra thick double (heavy) cream

3 tbsp brown sugar

1 Peel and slice the fresh fruit and put it in the bottom of a flameproof dish. Pour the peaches and their juice over and mix well.

2 In a separate bowl, mix the fromage frais, crème frâche or yoghurt with the cream.

3 Cover the fruit with the cream mixture and sprinkle the sugar over.

4 Get the grill (broiler) really hot and pop the dish under for a couple of minutes or until the sugar starts to bubble. Leave to cool just long enough to avoid blistering your mouth on scarily hot sugar, or leave to cool, then chill for not much more than 2 hours.

Puddings are fattening – you can't get away from it. But you can cut the calories in this recipe by using low-fat cream substitute, yoghurt or fromage frais instead of the double cream.

Fruit crumble

SERVES 4

4 handfuls of chopped fresh fruit (apples, plums, pears and rhubarb all work well)

About 3 tbsp sugar (less for sweet apples, more for cooking (tart) apples and rhubarb)

6 tbsp flour

8 tbsp margarine

4 tbsp sugar

2 tbsp muesli (optional)

TO SERVE:

Cream or custard

1 Put the fruit in a heatproof dish. Sprinkle sugar over to taste.

2 Put the remaining ingredients in a separate bowl and rub in with the fingertips (imagine a small blob of Blu-Tack in your fingers and you'll soon get the hang of it). Stop when the mixture looks like breadcrumbs.

3 Spoon this on top of the fruit and bake in a preheated oven at 190ºC/375ºF/gas 5/ fan oven 170ºC for at least 30–40 minutes. Crumble is very good-tempered so it will sit in the oven happily for longer if need be – just don't let it burn.

4 Serve with cream or custard (the best custard comes ready made in cartons – don't worry about making it yourself).

Experiment with different combinations of fruit – try raisins with apple, soft berry fruits with pear, or orange with rhubarb.

Trifle pudding

SERVES 4

½ an un-iced banana or
carrot loaf

Juice of 1 orange

A slug of sherry (optional)

3 bananas

3 small (150 ml/¼ pt/⅔ cup)
cartons of 'custard-style'
fruit yoghurt

A small (150 ml/¼ pt/⅔ cup)
carton of extra thick double
(heavy) cream

1 kiwi fruit, peeled and
sliced, or a little drinking
(sweetened) chocolate
powder (optional)

1 Slice the loaf thinly and line a bowl with it. Pour over the orange juice and sherry, if using, so the bread is well soaked.

2 Peel and slice the bananas, then sprinkle over the bread.

3 Pour the yoghurt over and top with the cream.

4 Decorate with kiwi fruit slices or a dusting of chocolate powder, if liked, just before serving.

TOP TIP

You can use sponge fingers instead
of banana or carrot loaf, or use up
any stale cake – in the unlikely event
that you have any!

Bread and butter pudding

SERVES 4

A small lump of margarine

4 slices of bread, buttered and quartered

A handful of dried mixed fruit (fruit cake mix)

3 eggs

600 ml/1 pt/2½ cups milk

4 tbsp sugar

1 Rub the margarine around a heatproof dish.

2 Arrange the bread in the bottom of the dish to line it completely.

3 Sprinkle the dried fruit over the bread.

4 Beat together the eggs, milk and sugar. Pour over the bread and leave to soak for 30 minutes (if you have time).

5 Bake in a preheated oven at 180°C/350°F/ gas 4/fan oven 160°C for 40 minutes or until the centre has set and the top is crisp and golden.

TOP TIP

For an extra treat, make this with brioche and chopped dried apricots.

Chocolate fondue

SERVES 4

A large bar (about 200 g/
7 oz) of plain (semi-sweet)
chocolate

A small (150 ml/¼ pt/⅔ cup)
carton of double (heavy)
cream

4 tbsp sherry

Fruit for dipping such as
orange segments,
strawberries, chunks of
banana, sliced pear, grapes

1 Break the chocolate into squares and put in a heatproof bowl with the cream and sherry.

2 Stand the bowl over a saucepan of gently simmering water and stir until the chocolate melts (don't let it get too hot or it will go grainy).

3 Give everyone a plate of fruit and a fork to make dipping easier. If the chocolate starts to solidify, pop it back on to the saucepan for a minute and stir well.

Cut fruit goes brown very quickly, so
leave chopping until the last minute or
sprinkle the fruit with lemon juice. The
lemon juice trick works for avocados too.

Baked stuffed peaches

SERVES 4

4 ripe peaches or a large (600 g/1¼ lb) can of peach halves in juice

A small (175 g/6 oz) carton of cream cheese

4 tbsp chopped mixed nuts

5 tbsp sugar

1 Carefully peel the peaches, halve and remove the stones (pits) or drain the juice from canned peaches.

2 Mix together the cheese, nuts and 1 tbsp of the sugar in a small bowl.

3 Stuff the cheese mixture into the hole in the peach where the stone was. Sprinkle the remaining sugar over the peaches.

4 Place the peach halves, stuffed-sides up, in a heatproof dish and bake in a preheated oven at 160°C/325°F/gas 3/fan oven 145°C for 10 minutes.

TOP TIP

For quickness, flash the peaches under a hot grill (broiler) for 2–3 minutes instead of baking them in the oven.

Banana loaf

SERVES 4

5 tbsp oil, plus extra for greasing

10 tbsp self-raising wholemeal flour

2 handfuls of raisins or sultanas (golden raisins)

2 heaped tbsp chopped mixed unsalted nuts

3 tbsp sugar

1 tsp baking powder

A pinch of salt

3 ripe bananas

2 eggs, beaten

Juice of 1 orange

TO SERVE:

Margarine for spreading (optional)

1 Grease a 450 g/1 lb loaf tin with a little oil.

2 Mix together the flour, fruit, nuts, sugar, baking powder and salt in a large bowl.

3 In a separate bowl, mash the bananas with a fork and beat in the eggs, oil and 5 tbsp of the orange juice (it won't look that great at this stage!). Pour this into the dry ingredients and mix well.

4 Spoon into the tin and bake in a preheated oven at 180°C/350°F/gas 4/fan oven 160°C for 45 minutes.

5 Cover with foil and cook for another 30 minutes or until cooked through.

6 Leave to cool slightly, then loosen the edge and turn out on to a wire rack to cool completely. Serve cut into slices and spread with margarine, if liked.

TOP TIP

If you don't have a loaf tin, a small cake tin or heatproof basin (about 18–20 cm/ 7–8 in in diameter) will do.

If you haven't a wire rack, use the grill pan rack or improvise with something else that will help the cake cool evenly. Try standing it on a line of knives or a couple of wire coat hangers, one laid on top of the other at an angle.

Banana bread pudding

SERVES 4

4 tbsp margarine

3 tbsp sugar

A small (150 ml/¼ pt/⅔ cup) carton of single (light) cream

4 slices of Banana Loaf (see page 92)

Vanilla ice-cream

1 Melt the margarine and sugar in a saucepan over a very low heat, stirring all the time.

2 When it's golden coloured (don't let it go brown), stir in the cream. Keep warm.

3 Toast the banana bread and put each slice on a plate. Top with ice-cream and pour the sauce over.

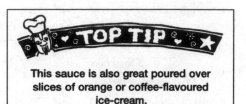

This sauce is also great poured over slices of orange or coffee-flavoured ice-cream.

All-in-one chocolate cake

SERVES 4

FOR THE CAKE:

Oil for greasing

8 tbsp self-raising flour, plus
extra for dusting

A small (75 g/3 oz) bar of
plain (semi-sweet) chocolate

A 250 g/9 oz block or tub of
margarine

8 tbsp sugar

3 tbsp milk

1½ tsp baking powder

4 tbsp cocoa (unsweetened
chocolate) powder

4 eggs, beaten

FOR THE ICING:

8 tbsp sugar

A large (200 g/7 oz) bar of
plain (semi-sweet) chocolate

6 tbsp milk

1 Make the cake first. Grease a 20 cm/8 in diameter cake tin with oil, then shake some flour around to dust it completely.

2 Melt the chocolate and margarine very slowly in a large saucepan. Switch off the heat and mix in the flour and all the other cake ingredients, adding the eggs last.

3 Pour into the tin and bake in a preheated oven at 180°C/350°F/gas 4/fan oven 160°C for 1 hour.

4 Put all the icing ingredients in a saucepan and melt together. Bring to the boil. Switch off the heat and leave to cool.

5 Once the cake is cooked, remove from the oven and leave to stand for 10 minutes.

6 Carefully turn out on to a wire rack (see page 92 if you haven't one) and leave to cool completely.

7 Cut the cake in half and sandwich back together with a little of the icing. Spread the remaining icing over the top and sides of the cake.

**Keep cakes wrapped in foil or in an
airtight tin.**

Nut and chocolate crunch

SERVES 4

Oil for greasing

8 tbsp margarine

A large (200 g/7 oz) bar of plain (semi-sweet) chocolate

16 (about 250 g/9 oz) digestive biscuits (graham crackers), crushed

A small bag (100 g/4 oz) of chopped mixed nuts

2 tbsp sugar

1 tbsp sherry or rum (optional)

A small (150 ml/¼ pt/⅔ cup) carton of double (heavy) cream

1 Lightly oil a 20 cm/8 in cake tin.

2 Melt the margarine in a large saucepan, add the chocolate and melt it over a very low heat.

3 Remove from the heat, stir in all the other ingredients and spoon into the cake tin. When cold, chill for at least 2 hours or until firm. Turn out and cut into wedges.

TOP TIP

If you're investing in a cake tin, get a deep one with a removable base.

Quick apple cake

SERVES 4

Oil for greasing

10 tbsp plain (all-purpose)
flour, plus extra for dusting

8 tbsp margarine

7 tbsp sugar

2 eggs, beaten

3 tsp baking powder

2 tbsp orange juice

4 eating apples, peeled,
cored and chopped

3 tbsp chopped walnuts

1 Grease a 20 cm/8 in diameter cake tin with oil, then shake some flour around to dust it completely.

2 Melt the margarine in a large saucepan, beat in 5 tbsp of the sugar and beat with a wooden spoon or a balloon whisk until the mixture is pale and creamy.

3 Mix in the eggs, flour, baking powder and orange juice, then stir in the chopped apples.

4 Pour into the tin. Spread the walnuts over the top of the cake and sprinkle the remaining sugar on top.

5 Bake in a preheated oven at 160°C/ 325°F/gas 3/fan oven 145°C for about 1 hour until the centre springs back when lightly pressed and the top is golden. Remove from the oven and leave to stand for 10 minutes.

A cake is cooked when a sharp knife pushed into the middle comes out clean.

11 Ready to party

A little advance planning will ensure your parties are the ones your guests will still be talking about 10 years later. If you want your party to be great, then you need to work out a game plan. Should it be fancy dress or have a theme? What time to you want it to start? Who provides the booze? Getting the alcoholic content of a party right is vital – you want everyone to have a good time without throwing up all over your bathroom. Plus, think about how many people you can realistically invite and not wreck the house. Never fall into the trap of putting an open invitation on the internet!

Make sure everyone knows they are expected to bring some drink, and buy a bag of plastic 'glasses' from the pound shop.

If you are feeling very organised, plan to have a punch and suggest to guests what sort of drink they should bring. You'll need a clean bucket or large washing up bowl, about five bottles of cold white wine, three litres of orange juice and a bottle of cheap brandy. This should keep 10–15 people happy, so multiply according to the guest list. Add some chopped fresh fruit to make it look like you've put in some effort and provide soft drinks for drivers and non-drinkers.

Some more party ideas:

- Fancy dress can be a laugh: try toffs and chavs, anything that begins with the letter H (or any other letter), angels and devils, the sixties, James Bond, the jungle…

- Try a salsa party: beg, borrow or steal lambada tapes, buy in Mexican beer and set up a tequila bouncer on the door. The bouncer has to give everyone a traditional tequila shot – a lick of salt on the back of the hand, a shot of tequila and a slice of lime or lemon to bite on.

Stay ahead of the game by drinking lots of water on the night – it really will help prevent a hangover the next day. And don't forget to eat as well as drink.

- Vodka jelly is another conversation piece: break two packets of lime jelly into cubes and dissolve in a little boiling water, then add 600 ml/1 pt/2½ cups of vodka. Pour into ice cube trays and chill (it will take a while to set, so start early).

Do try to keep drinks cold – it makes a big difference. Clear out the fridge and pack it with booze. Even better, see if a tame medical student can get you a sack of ice (don't ask where from) and fill the bath with it. If that fails, stand bottles in buckets of cold water in the garden if you have one. At worst, use the bath!

- If it's Christmas or New Year, try glühwein: simmer 600 ml/1 pt/2½ cups of orange juice with two cinnamon sticks, a handful of cloves and 4 tbsp of sugar for 10 minutes, then strain. In a big saucepan, heat one bottle of cheap red wine, 600 ml/1 pt/2½ cups of water, a large slug of brandy and a ladleful of the orange syrup. Alternatively, buy glühwein sachets (they look like teabags) and follow the instructions on the packet.

A word of warning

Student parties are notorious for good reasons. They're easy to crash and easy to trash. Keep an eye on who knows about your party beforehand and who's coming in on the night. If necessary, get a burly mate to stand on the door and check invitations. You don't want to be the ones losing your deposit on the house or talking to the police at 2 in the morning if things get out of hand.

Do warn your neighbours if it's going to be a biggie, because you don't want them calling the police. It's even worth inviting them.

Don't forget to stock up on loo paper when doing your party shopping!

They probably won't come, but if invited they're less likely to complain.

As I said before, never put an open invitation online.

The food

If you're asking guests not to turn up until 10 pm or so, it's fair to expect them to have eaten before they arrive. But that means you get the dreaded post-pub crowd, so

Make bulk-bought cheap crisps more exciting by serving them with a dip (see page 101). Check out ethnic shops for interesting snacks.

it can be a good idea to get people to pitch up a bit earlier and then provide them with some food to soak up the alcohol. Of course, this makes the party more expensive, but it also makes it more of an event and is a good excuse to limit numbers.

Party food divides into two varities – easy-to-eat-with-the-fingers nibbles and huge servings of easily prepared nosh.

Nibbles

Aim for about eight nibbles per person.

Mini pizzas

Mini pitta breads

Tomato purée (paste)

Dried mixed herbs

Sliced mushrooms

Grated cheese

1 Toast the pitta breads on one side.

2 Spread tomato purée on the other side and top with herbs, mushrooms, then the cheese.

3 Grill (broil) for about 4 minutes or until the cheese is bubbling. These taste fine cold.

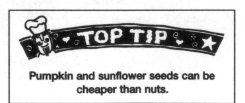

Pumpkin and sunflower seeds can be cheaper than nuts.

Tortilla chips, cheese and salsa

SERVES 8

A big bag of tortilla chips

A jar of salsa sauce

4 handfuls of grated cheese

1 Put the chips on a flameproof plate or in a shallow bowl.

2 Spread the salsa over the top and sprinkle on the cheese.

3 Grill (broil) for about 3 minutes. Serve at once.

Mini meatballs

MAKES ABOUT 20

450 g/1 lb minced (ground) beef

1 egg, beaten

1 garlic clove, peeled and crushed

1 tbsp tomato purée (paste)

1 tsp dried mixed herbs

Oil

TO SERVE:

Dips (see opposite) and wooden cocktail sticks

1 Mix together the beef, egg, garlic, tomato purée and herbs in a bowl. Roll into about 20 little balls.

2 Heat a little oil in a frying pan and fry the balls for about 5 minutes, turning until browned all over. Serve with a dip.

Dust your hands with a little flour before you roll the meatballs to stop the mixture sticking to your hands.

Curry sauce dip

A small (150 ml/¼ pt/⅔ cup) carton of plain yoghurt

A small (150 ml/¼ pt/⅔ cup) carton of double (heavy) cream

2 tbsp mayonnaise

1 or 2 tsp curry powder (depending on your taste)

1 Mix everything together well.

2 Serve chilled.

Cucumber dip

2 small (150 ml/¼ pt/⅔ cup) cartons of plain yoghurt

½ cucumber, grated

1 garlic clove, crushed

1 Mix everything together well.

2 Serve chilled.

Tomato dip

1 onion, finely chopped

1 tbsp oil

A large (400 g/14 oz) can of chopped tomatoes with garlic and herbs

1 tsp dried mixed herbs

1 Fry the onion in the oil until transparent.

2 Add the tomatoes and herbs and simmer for 5 minutes.

3 Allow to cool before serving.

Large-scale party nosh

If you don't want to cook, simply provide loads of French bread, slabs of cheese and perhaps a few pickles.

Make sure you have enough plates and cutlery for everyone – borrow like mad or splash out on paper plates to make the clearing up operation less painful.

You can feed a lot of people quite cheaply by bulking out the dishes with lots of stodge – pasta, potatoes, etc. – but if the cost is prohibitive, consider asking people to contribute a couple of quid.

Two salmon pasta salad

SERVES 10

10 handfuls of pasta shapes

Salt

A large (about 400 g/14 oz) can of red or pink salmon

A small packet of smoked salmon trimmings

A small (150 ml/¼ pt/⅔ cup) carton of plain yoghurt

5 tbsp mayonnaise

5 tbsp double (heavy) cream

1 garlic clove, crushed

A small bunch of fresh dill (dill weed), chopped

TO SERVE:

A green salad and lots of fresh bread

1 Cook the pasta in plenty of boiling salted water according to the packet directions (use two pans if necessary). Drain and rinse with cold water.

2 Drain the can of salmon and chop the smoked salmon, removing any bones or skin from both.

3 Mix the salmon and all the remaining ingredients into the pasta really well. Serve with a green salad and fresh bread.

TOP TIP

If you are strapped for cash, leave out the smoked salmon, although it does taste good and trimmings are much cheaper than slices.

Coronation chicken

SERVES 10

1.75 kg/4 lb oven-ready chicken (completely thawed if frozen)

6 tbsp mayonnaise

5 tbsp double (heavy) cream

3 tbsp mango chutney

2 tsp curry powder

2 handfuls of sultanas (golden raisins) or raisins

TO SERVE:

A green salad and Rice Salad (see below)

1 Roast the chicken for 1 hour 40 minutes (see page 23). Leave to cool. (This can be done the day before – but remember to keep the chicken in the fridge.)

2 Remove the skin from the chicken and take off as much meat as you can. Chop it up and mix with all the other ingredients.

3 Serve with a green salad and Rice Salad.

Rice salad

SERVES 10

10 handfuls of long-grain rice

Salt

2 handfuls of frozen peas

1 red or green (bell) pepper, finely chopped

A small (200 g/7 oz) can of sweetcorn, drained

4 tbsp olive oil

2 tbsp vinegar

Salt and pepper

1 Boil the rice in plenty of salted water for 10 minutes or until just tender. Add the peas for the last 5 minutes of cooking.

2 Drain and rinse with cold water.

3 Put in a serving bowl and mix in all the other ingredients. Season with salt and pepper.

Classy chilli

SERVES 10
Double the quantities for the Cheap Chilli on page 65. Using two pans if necessary, cook 10 handfuls of rice (see page 21 or Rice Salad, page 103). Drain, rinse with hot water and drain again. Serve hot with bowls of garnishes, such as:

- finely chopped lettuce and tomato salad
- a large carton of soured (dairy sour) cream or plain yoghurt
- a bowl of grated Cheddar cheese
- tortilla chips
- Avocado Dip (see page 51)

Vegetarian chilli

SERVES 10

2 onions, chopped

3 tbsp oil

2 garlic cloves, chopped

2 aubergines (eggplants), cubed

2 courgettes (zucchini), thickly sliced

A large (350 g/12 oz) can of sweetcorn, drained

2 large (425 g/15 oz) cans of red kidney beans in chilli sauce

A large (400 g/14 oz) can of chopped tomatoes

Chilli powder to taste

1 Fry the onions in the oil until transparent.

2 Add the garlic, aubergines and courgettes and fry for 2–3 minutes.

3 Add all the other ingredients and simmer for 20 minutes. Serve as Classy Chilli (see above), using vegetarian Cheddar.

Chicken and cauliflower curry

SERVES 10

2 onions, chopped

3 tbsp oil

2 garlic cloves, chopped

4 tbsp curry powder

20 boneless chicken thighs

A large (300 ml/½ pt/1¼ cup) carton of double (heavy) cream

2 handfuls of red lentils

2 large (400 g/14 oz) cans of chopped tomatoes

1 large cauliflower, broken into small florets

TO SERVE:

Rice (see Classy Chilli, page 104), mango chutney and Cucumber Dip (see page 101)

1 Fry the onions in the oil until transparent.

2 Add the garlic, curry powder and chicken and fry, stirring, for 5 minutes.

3 Add all the remaining ingredients except the cauliflower, cover and cook gently for 20 minutes.

4 Add the cauliflower. Cook, uncovered, for another 10 minutes.

5 Serve with rice, mango chutney and Cucumber Dip.

TOP TIP

Taste your curry near the end of cooking and, if it's not hot enough, add chilli powder rather than curry powder – curry powder needs time to cook properly to release its flavour.

Vegetable curry

SERVES 10

2 onions, chopped

3 tbsp oil

2 garlic cloves, chopped

6 large potatoes, diced

10 handfuls of spinach, washed and torn into pieces

4 tbsp curry powder

2 large (400 g/14 oz) cans of chopped tomatoes

2 tbsp lemon juice

TO SERVE:

Plain yoghurt, rice (see Classy Chilli, page 104) and popadoms

1 Fry the onions in the oil until transparent, then add all the remaining ingredients.

2 Cook, uncovered, for 20 minutes.

3 Serve with yoghurt, rice and poppadoms.

If your curry is too hot, stir in some yoghurt or cream to cool it down.

The morning after

So it was a party never to be forgotten, which is strange as you can't remember most of it. The house looks like a bombsite and the inside of your head feels like one. Grab a bin liner each, get The Slacker out of bed and give him/her the vacuum cleaner and clear up NOW. Within half an hour everything will look a whole lot better (I promise) and you can contemplate curing your hangover. The best way to do this is with a big fry up. It's one of the most difficult things to time right, but follow this minute-by-minute guide and you can't go wrong.

Fry up

SERVES 4

8 chipolata sausages or veggie bangers

8 rashers (slices) of bacon (or hash browns for veggies)

2 large (420 g/15 oz) cans of baked beans

Oil

4 handfuls of sliced mushrooms

Salt and pepper

A pinch of dried mixed herbs

8 slices of bread

8 eggs

Tea and coffee

The countdown

Minus 15 minutes: Assemble the ingredients, fill the kettle, switch on the grill (broiler) to medium and the oven to 160°C/325°F/gas 3/fan oven 145°C.

Minus 14: Place the sausages in the centre of the grill (broiler) pan and half the bacon/hash browns round the edge (don't worry if the bacon overlaps – it will shrink). Start cooking.

Minus 12: Open the beans and put them in a saucepan ready to go on the cooker. Check on the bacon and sausages – turn if necessary.

Minus 11: Heat about 2 tbsp of oil in a large pan. Fry the mushrooms, season with salt and pepper and a pinch of herbs, turn into a heatproof bowl and place in the bottom of the oven to keep warm. Check the bacon and sausages – turn the sausages again if necessary.

Minus 10: Once cooked, put the bacon/hash browns in the oven to keep warm and put the rest on the grill (leave the sausages as they will take longer).

Minus 9: Put the kettle on and the first round of toast in the toaster.

Minus 8: Put the first round of toast in the oven, along with all the plates.

Minus 6: Put on more toast. Put 2–3 tbsp of oil into the frying pan and crack in four eggs. Push the whites together to stop them spreading.

Minus 4: Put the second round of toast in the oven and start another lot. Check on the grill. Get someone else to make the tea and coffee, get the cutlery and find the ketchup.

Minus 3: Put the first lot of eggs in the oven and start the rest. Ditto toast. Put the heat on under the beans.

Minus 2: Get the warm plates and food out of the oven (use an oven glove) and start dividing up. By the time you've done this, the other eggs, the toast and the beans will be ready.

Zero hour: Sit down and get stuck in.

If you really feel so bad after your party that you can't face an onslaught of fat and washing up, then drink lots of water, take a painkiller and a vitamin C tablet and try one of the alternative pick-you-ups below. They all serve one.

Fruit shake: Mash a banana in a bowl. Add the juice of two oranges and mix well. Pour into a glass and add ice cubes.

Porridge: Half-fill a mug with porridge oats. Put the oats in a saucepan. Fill the mug with milk or water and pour into the pan. Sprinkle in some raisins, if you have some. Heat gently, stirring all the time, for 3–4 minutes. Alternatively, make Hot Muesli (see page 32).

Dried fruit: Pour a glass of orange juice into a saucepan. Add a large handful of dried fruit (pear, apple, prunes, etc.). Bring to the boil, then simmer for 15 minutes.

12 Entertaining

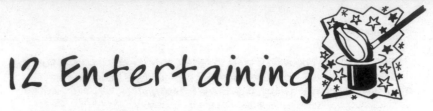

If all this talk of parties sounds a little too raucous for you, then how about inviting your mates to an elegant dinner party? This involves feeding between six and ten friends with your best recipes and them sitting down, rather than standing up, to get drunk.

Before you even start to think about what to cook consider these questions.

- **Do I invite my housemates?** If not, how are you going to ask them politely to get lost while you entertain more favoured friends? If yes, how many others do you have room for?

- **Do I have enough cutlery, crockery and chairs for everyone?** If you're serving soup and a pudding you'll need a lot of bowls and spoons. Or can you face breaking off in the middle to wash up?

- **Am I going to be able to cook everything on my own, or do I need to enlist a willing helper?** (Try to get someone else to wash up!)

Menu planning

When you're happy with the logistics you can plan a menu. As you decide on your menu, make a time plan too. Decide when you intend to start eating and work backwards from there. If you find your menu is too complicated, plan another one. The last thing you want is to be juggling in the kitchen while your guests are having a great time without you.

Stir-fries make good dinner party main courses. Stick to just three main ingredients – mushrooms, red (bell) peppers and meat, for example.

- Keep the menu varied – each course should have different flavours and textures. Don't go for dairy product overkill – for instance, creamy mushroom soup, followed by pasta with cream, leek and bacon sauce, then fruit brûlée.

- Don't be afraid to serve old favourites like curry and chilli – just jazz them up a bit with side dishes (see Chapter 11 on pages 97–106). All sorts of recipes can be upgraded with a bit of thought – extra cream, spices, fresh herbs and slightly better-quality ingredients can make all the difference.

Here are some suggested menus to delight your guests, gathered from the recipes in this book. Increase quantities of ingredients according to numbers. Each has a rough time guide to help you.

Menu 1 (vegetarian)

Veggie Sticks and Avocado Dip (see page 51).
Bump up the chilli powder to make it spicier and serve with tortilla chips as well as the veggie sticks.

Spinach and Mushroom Pasta (see page 39)
Add a small can of stoned (pitted) olives, drained and chopped. Serve with salad.

Banana Bread Pudding (see page 93)

Time plan

Earlier that day: Cut the carrots, cucumbers, peppers, etc. into matchsticks for the dip. Keep them covered in the fridge. Make the Banana Loaf (or buy some) and the sauce.

1 hour to go: Make the pasta sauce. Measure the pasta into a saucepan and fill the kettle. Prepare all the ingredients for the dip except the avocado and put in a serving bowl. Make the salad and dressing, but keep separate.

Just before serving: Add the avocado to the dip ingredients. Cook the pasta. Reheat the sauce. Assemble the salad. Assemble the pudding.

Menu 2

Greek starter
Serve shop-bought houmous and taramasalata with Cucumber Dip (see page 101), chunks of cucumber and olives and warm pitta bread cut into fingers.

Chicken in a Pot (see page 72)
Serve with baked potatoes (see page 22) and a green vegetable such as broccoli.

All-in-one Chocolate Cake (see page 94) or *Nut and Chocolate Crunch* (see page 95)
Serve with a sauce made by pushing a can of raspberries and their juice through a sieve (strainer).

Time plan
Earlier that day: Prepare the chicken so it's completely ready to go in the oven. Make the cake and sauce.

1 hour to go: Put the chicken and potatoes in the preheated oven. Prepare the green vegetable and put in a saucepan.

Just before serving: Assemble the starter. Steam or boil the green vegetables. Assemble the pudding.

Menu 3 (vegetarian)

Hot and Spicy Tofu Salad (see page 43)
Leave out the sweetcorn.

Cheese and Aubergine Pie (see page 73)
Substitute the Cheddar with a small pack of Mozzarella cheese, chopped, and a small slab of Emmental (Swiss) cheese, grated. Serve with pasta shapes tossed in olive oil or margarine and fresh herbs.

Quick Apple Cake (see page 96)
Serve with shop-bought apple sauce and crème fraîche or fromage frais.

Time plan
Earlier that day: Make the pie up to the point when it goes into the oven. Make the cake.

1 hour to go: Marinate the tofu. Assemble the salad ingredients. Put the pasta in the saucepan and fill the kettle.

Just before serving: Cook the Tofu Salad. Cook the pasta. Assemble the pudding.

Menu 4

French Onion Soup (see page 55)
Substitute the stock cubes and water with 2 medium (275 g/10 oz) cans of consommé (clear beef soup) and 3 tbsp of cheap dry sherry. Use slices of French stick rather than ordinary bread.

Creamy Leek and Bacon Pasta (see page 37)
Serve with salad.

Trifle Pudding (see page 88)
Top with slices of kiwi fruit or strawberries.

Time plan

Earlier that day: Make the pudding and store in the fridge.

1 hour to go: Make the pasta sauce. Put the pasta in a saucepan so it's ready to go. Make up the soup to the point where you toast the bread. Assemble the salad ingredients.

Just before serving: Finish the soup. Cook the pasta and reheat the sauce. Pour the dressing on to the salad.

Menu 5 (suitable for vegans)

Bread and Bean Soup (see page 57)

Thai Vegetable Curry (see page 74)
Try to include some chopped fresh coriander (cilantro).

Baked Stuffed Peaches (see page 91)
Use a soya-based cream 'cheese'.

Time plan

Earlier that day: Make the soup up to the point when you add the bread.

1 hour to go: Make the curry, but don't add the coriander. Prepare the pudding.

Just before serving: Finish the soup. Reheat the curry and add the coriander. Don't put boiling water on the noodles until just before serving. Preheat the grill (broiler), then cook the pudding.

Menu 6 (vegetarian)

Saucy Mushrooms (see page 54)
Crumble over some blue-veined cheese suitable for vegetarians.

Vegetable Puff Pie (see page 80)
Serve with salad or with green vegetables and boiled potatoes.

Fruit Salad Brûlée (see page 86)

Time plan

Earlier that day: Make the pie and pudding.

1 hour to go: Assemble the Saucy Mushrooms ingredients. Prepare the potatoes and salad/vegetables. Preheat the oven.

Just before serving: Make the Saucy Mushrooms and the toast. Put the potatoes on to boil and put the pie in the oven.

Menu 7

Spinach, Bacon and Avocado Salad (see page 43)
Don't use too many ingredients in the salad base – just lettuce would be okay.

Stuffed Trout (see page 75)
Serve with boiled potatoes and broccoli.

Bread and Butter Pudding (see page 89)
Slice a banana, toss in lemon juice and sandwich between the bread.
Substitute 150 ml/¼ pt/⅔ cup of double (heavy) cream for the same quantity of milk and add 2 tbsp of sherry or brandy.

Time plan

Earlier that day: Prepare the trout. Assemble the pudding but don't cook it.

1 hour to go: Preheat the oven. Prepare the potatoes and broccoli. Fry the bacon.

Just before serving: Assemble the salad, put the fish and pudding into the oven at the same time. Boil the potatoes and cook the broccoli.

Menu 8

Goats' Cheese and Grilled Pepper Salad (see page 44)
Use slices from a French stick as the base for the cheese.

Pork Casserole (see page 84)
Use cider instead of the apple juice. Serve with mangetout (snow peas) instead of the greens.

Fruit Crumble (see page 87)
Serve with cream.

Time plan

Earlier that day: Grill (broil) the peppers and leave to marinate in the dressing. Assemble the casserole and put into the fridge. Make the crumble topping.

1 hour to go: Put the casserole and potatoes into the preheated oven. Assemble the pudding.

Just before serving: Finish the salad and put the pudding into the oven. Cook the vegetables.

Menu 9

Noodle Soup (see page 56)
Use a small bag of defrosted prawns (shrimp) or stick to one vegetable and add some fresh coriander.

Stuffed Chicken Breasts (see page 77)
Serve with French Potatoes (see page 78) and a green vegetable.

Chocolate Fondue (see page 90)

Time plan

Earlier that day: Prepare the chicken breasts and put in the fridge. Peel the potatoes and leave completely covered in cold water so they don't go brown. Defrost the prawns.

1 hour to go: Preheat the oven. Start cooking the potatoes. Make the fondue.

Just before serving: Put the chicken in the oven. Make the soup. Prepare the fruit for the fondue.

Menu 10 (vegetarian)

Tortilla Chips, Cheese and Salsa (see page 100)

Vegetable Goulash (see page 76)
Serve with rice.

Mars Bar Sauce and Ice-cream (see page 85)

Time plan

Earlier that day: Make the goulash.

1 hour to go: Grate the cheese. Make the Mars Bar Sauce.

Just before serving: Cook the rice. Assemble the starter. Reheat the goulash and add the soured cream. Reheat the sauce and assemble the pudding.

Dinner party dos and don'ts

Do:

- Prepare as much food as you can in advance.
- Ask guests to bring booze – but buy some yourself in case there isn't enough.
- Chill white wine.
- Check that your corkscrew works.
- Provide mineral water or a jug of iced tap water.
- Leave yourself plenty of time to get the food and yourself ready – it's bound to take longer than you think.
- Put candles on the table and play music.

Don't:

- Run out of milk for coffee.
- Apologise if things go wrong.
- Skimp on quantities.
- Cut the bread or dress the salad until the last minute.
- Panic!

Sunday lunches

Dinner parties don't have to happen in the evenings. Why not invite people around for Sunday lunch like mum makes? They'll love you for ever.

Every good Sunday lunch needs:

- a roast or casserole
- stuffing
- gravy
- a sauce or relish
- roast potatoes
- at least two different vegetables
- a stodgy pudding

The roast: You'll need a deep roasting tin to sit the meat or chicken in. Follow the cooking instructions on pages 22–23. Add some chopped onion or dried mixed herbs to the pan for flavour. If you're unsure what sort of meat will roast well, look at the guidelines on supermarket packets, but loin, shoulder or leg are always good bets. When the meat or chicken is cooked, let is rest for about 10 minutes. This makes it easier to carve and gives you time to make the gravy – gravy granules are quick and easy. If you are cooking vegetarian, make the deluxe stuffing below, or the nut roast mixes you can buy in supermarkets and health food shops are very easy (and you can jazz them up with extra ingredients).

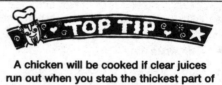

A chicken will be cooked if clear juices run out when you stab the thickest part of the leg with a sharp knife. If they look at all pink, it needs longer in the oven.

Casseroles: These are a good alternative to a roast. Try Pork Casserole (see page 84) or Fruity Bean Stew (see page 67).

Stuffing: This can be made from a packet or with breadcrumbs, melted margarine and flavourings like chopped onion, herbs, lemon juice and chopped apple. Stuffing can be baked separately in a small heatproof dish. If you're cooking for vegetarians as well as meat-eaters, make lots of deluxe stuffing out of wholemeal breadcrumbs, chopped onion, melted butter, a glass of wine, chopped dried apricots and nuts. Serve it as an alternative to the meat.

Gravy: This is the home-made way! Once the meat is cooked, put it on a large plate and leave to rest. Spoon off and discard all but a couple of tablespoonfuls of the fat from the roasting tin (leave the juices) and put the tin on the hob. Sprinkle in 2 tbsp of flour and stir for about 4 minutes or until it's really brown. Add 450 ml/¾ pt/2 cups of water (preferably from cooking the vegetables) and cook until thick. Make vegetarian gravy by frying a chopped onion in 1 tbsp of oil. Add 1 tbsp of flour, crumble in a veggie stock cube, then stir in the water and 1 tbsp of tomato purée (paste). Alternatively, reach for the granules.

Sauces: Each type of meat has a traditional accompaniment and they can all be bought virtually ready-made. Bread sauce for chicken, apple sauce for pork, mint sauce or redcurrant jelly (clear conserve) for lamb and cranberry sauce for turkey.

Potatoes and vegetables: Follow the instructions on pages 21 and 23 and don't skimp on quantities – everyone will eat at least five roasties. Oven-baked vegetables will cook alongside the roast – try sliced aubergine (eggplant), courgettes (zucchini) and (bell) peppers with a little crushed garlic and olive oil, cooked in a roasting tin; or shredded red cabbage with raisins, a chopped apple, some sugar, a little water and a dash of vinegar cooked in a casserole dish (Dutch oven) with a lid.

Pudding: Classic puddings to follow a roast are Bread and Butter Pudding (see page 89), Fruit Crumble (see page 87) and Trifle Pudding (see page 88). Serve with shop-bought custard, cream or ice-cream.

Timings

The hardest thing about cooking a roast is timing everything so it all comes together at the end. Work backwards from the time you want to dish up. Anything that's been cooked in the oven will sit there on a low heat quite happily, so don't panic if you get it a bit wrong. Leave green vegetables and gravy until the last minute – prepare the ingredients and boil a kettle, then cook them while someone else carves and dishes up the rest of the food.

13 Leftovers

There are two types of leftovers – the small amount of food left after a meal and the large amount of term left after the money's run out. Both call for drastic measures.

Leftover food

The majority of food that gets left is stodgy – mashed potato, rice and pasta.

- The easiest thing to do with cold rice or pasta is to turn it into a salad with some dressing and anything else you have to hand – chopped cucumber, tomatoes, sweetcorn, tuna, canned pulses, etc.

- Mashed potato can be covered with grated cheese and grilled, or warmed gently in the oven and topped with a fried egg.

- Reheat rice and pasta by shoving it into a colander or sieve (strainer) and steaming it over a saucepan of boiling water for 4–5 minutes, stirring occasionally.

- Cooked rice can be stir-fried in oil with other bits and pieces you may have knocking about – chopped cooked bacon, a few prawns (shrimp), chopped onion, cooked peas, chopped garlic, etc. When it's thoroughly heated

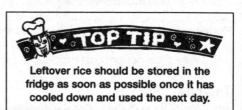

Leftover rice should be stored in the fridge as soon as possible once it has cooled down and used the next day.

through, push it to one side of the pan and pour a couple of beaten eggs into the space. Scramble them lightly, then mix in with the rice. Add a dash of soy sauce and – hey! – you've made special fried rice.

- Use leftover cooked vegetables or salad (including dressing) to make a soup with boiling water, a crumbled stock cube, soy sauce and noodles.

- Freeze leftover meat dishes for another day – or deliberately make extra to freeze and save cooking.

- Spice up boiled eggs or cooked meat with a curry sauce made by frying a chopped onion, a chopped apple and 1 tbsp of curry powder in a little oil. Add 1 tbsp of flour and stir. Add 300 ml/½ pt/1¼ cups of water, a small (200 g/7 oz) can of chopped tomatoes and 1 tsp of lemon juice. Simmer for 10 minutes, then add 1 tbsp of plain yoghurt if you have any.

Leftover term

When the money somehow seems to have run out, look to your store cupboard. You probably have at least 10 meals staring you in the face right there. But if the cupboard really is bare, call home, see your Student Union Welfare Officer or your bank – no one should go hungry.

If there is *something* in the cupboard, try the following recipes – they won't win Michelin stars but, as my mother says, they'll keep the wolf from the door.

Potato nests

SERVES 4

4 large potatoes, cut up

A dash of milk

Margarine

Salt and pepper

1 tbsp pesto sauce or 1 tbsp tomato ketchup (catsup) or 1 tsp made mustard

Oil

4 eggs

1 Boil the potatoes in boiling salted water until tender.

2 Mash them with the milk, margarine, salt and pepper and whichever flavouring you have to hand.

3 Oil a heatproof dish and put the mash in it. Make four little wells in the potato and break an egg into each one.

4 Bake in a preheated oven at 200°C/ 400°F/gas 6/fan oven 180°C for 10 minutes or until the eggs are set to your liking.

TOP TIP

Frozen bags of sausages, chicken breasts and other meat are much cheaper than those in the chill cabinet.

Pancakes

SERVES 4

4 tbsp plain (all-purpose) flour

1 egg

300 ml/½ pt/1¼ cup milk

Oil

Grated cheese or sugar and lemon juice

1 Put the flour in a bowl. Make a well in the centre.

2 Add the egg and half the milk.

3 Gradually draw the flour into the liquid, beating as you go, until you have a thick batter. Add the rest of the milk. (The batter can be left covered in the fridge for up to 24 hours before cooking.)

4 Heat a very little oil in a non-stick frying pan and pour off the excess. Add the batter 1 tbsp at a time, swirling the pan as you go. The secret of making pancakes is to put in as little batter as humanly possible (usually 2 tbsp). Loosen the sides with a fish slice and toss with a dramatic flourish. Cook the underside briefly. Then repeat until all the batter is used.

5 Serve rolled up with cheese or with sugar and lemon juice.

TOP TIP

Powdered sauces make a cheap stand-by to mix in with whatever you have to hand. They keep for ages, too.

Carrot and Marmite soup

SERVES 4

2 tbsp oil

3 onions, chopped

4 carrots, grated

4 handfuls of red lentils

900 ml/1½ pts/3¾ cups water

1 stock cube

2 tsp Marmite or other yeast extract

1 Heat the oil in a saucepan and fry the onions until transparent.

2 Add the carrots, lentils and water and crumble in the stock cube. Simmer for 20 minutes.

3 Stir in the Marmite and serve.

Pea pasta

SERVES 4

4 handfuls of pasta

Salt

4 handfuls of frozen peas

A small (200 g/7 oz) can of tuna, drained

3 tbsp mayonnaise or double (heavy) cream

Pepper

1 Cook the pasta in plenty of boiling salted water according to the packet directions. Add the peas for the last 5 minutes of cooking.

2 Drain the pasta quickly, then mix in the tuna and mayonnaise or cream. Season with pepper.

Multi-packs of cans are cheaper than buying individually.

Peanut noodles

SERVES 4

4 blocks of quick-cook egg noodles

4 tbsp peanut butter

4 tbsp soy sauce

1 tbsp vinegar

1 tsp sugar

1 Cook the noodles in boiling water according to the packet directions.

2 Put all the remaining ingredients in a small pan and heat gently so the peanut butter melts.

3 Drain the noodles and mix in the sauce. Serve straight away.

A spoonful of pesto stirred into cooked pasta or rice is a great stand-by. Or stir in a knob of butter and a handful of grated cheese.

Pauper's risotto

SERVES 4

6 handfuls of rice

A lump of margarine

1 tbsp grated Parmesan cheese

1 tbsp tomato purée (paste) (optional)

Anything else you have around – frozen vegetables, grated carrot, canned pulses, tuna, etc.

1 Cook the rice in plenty of boiling salted water for 20 minutes or until just tender.

2 Drain and stir in the margarine, cheese and tomato purée, if using. Add any extra ingredients, heat through and serve.

Own-brand potato powder is a cheap and useful stand-by and ideal if you don't have potatoes. It can also be used to thicken soups and sauces.

122

Vegetable crumble

SERVES 4

4 handfuls of any chopped
vegetables – carrot, potato,
courgette (zucchini),
aubergine (eggplant),
cabbage, etc.

A large (400 g/14 oz) can of
chopped tomatoes

1 tsp dried mixed herbs

8 tbsp plain (all-purpose)
flour

4 tbsp margarine

Salt and pepper

1 Simmer the vegetables with the tomatoes and herbs for 15 minutes in a covered pan.

2 Put the flour in a bowl with the margarine. Season well with salt and pepper.

3 Rub the fat into the flour with your fingertips as if rolling a small ball of Blu-Tack. Stop when the mixture looks like breadcrumbs.

4 Put the tomato mixture into a heatproof dish and top with the crumble mix.

5 Bake in a preheated oven at 190°C/375°F/ gas 5/fan oven 170°C for 30 minutes until the top is golden brown.

TOP TIP

Own-brand instant noodles are a mega-
cheap student staple. Serve them with
anything, or flavour with pesto, grated
cheese or any other sauces.

Chilli cabbage pasta

SERVES 4

4 handfuls of pasta shapes

1 small cabbage, de-stalked and shredded

½ tsp chilli powder (or more if you like)

2 tbsp grated Parmesan cheese

3 tbsp olive oil

1 Cook the pasta in plenty of boiling salted water according to the packet directions. Add the cabbage for the last 4 minutes of cooking.

2 Drain, stir in the remaining ingredients and serve.

Lentil soup with rice

SERVES 4

4 handfuls of rice

3 onions, sliced into rings

2 tbsp oil

A large (400 g/14 oz) can of lentil soup

2 tbsp curry powder

1 Cook the rice in plenty of boiling salted water for 10 minutes or until just tender. Drain.

2 Fry the onions slowly in the oil until golden.

3 Heat the soup with the curry powder. Serve the rice with the soup poured over and topped with the fried onions.

Stale bread salad

SERVES 4

8 slices of stale (but not mouldy!) bread

½ cucumber or 1 courgette (zucchini), chopped

4 tomatoes, chopped

1 (bell) pepper, seeded and chopped

1 tsp dried mixed herbs

4 tbsp olive oil

2 tbsp vinegar

Salt and pepper

1 Remove the crusts from the bread, then soak the slices for a few minutes in enough cold water to cover them. Squeeze out the excess water.

2 Put the bread in a bowl and mash with a fork.

3 Add all the remaining ingredients and mix well.

Onion pizza

SERVES 4

Home-made pizza ingredients (see page 79)

2 onions, sliced

Oil

1 If you made the pizza recipe in this book when you had more money, then you'll probably have the necessary flour and yeast left in the cupboard. Make up a pizza base as in the recipe, cover it with fried onions, and bake in a preheated oven at 200°C/400°F/gas 6/fan oven 180°C for 10 minutes until the base is cooked.

Index